PENGUIN SELF-STARTERS

Secretarial Skills

Gail Cornish was born and brought up in London and has worked as a senior secretary for over twenty years. Her experience spans all aspects of secretarial work, from temporary through to the presentation of plays, film and television scripts, university theses, to organizing and running senior management offices and devising office systems. Since having her two children she has worked freelance, both through her co-author's (Joan Lipkin-Edwards') agency and on her own. She writes her own scripts, books and plays.

Charlotte Coudrille has worked in many offices – as secretary, temporary secretary, office manager, administrator, as well as running a secretarial business from home – and sees the secretarial role as the keystone of the office. She has been working with office technology since the early days of microcomputers and has a great deal of experience in word-processing and keyboard training. She is currently involved in research and development of typing training on microcomputers, and has a special interest in electronic publishing.

Joan Lipkin-Edwards was born and educated in North-west London. She runs a secretarial, word-processing and conference staffing agency specializing in former top secretaries who, after breaking off to have families, now work part time or full time according to their commitments. Joan, who speaks several languages, trained as a secretary after leaving school and sets very high standards indeed for secretarial work, both for herself and for her workers. Her many years of dealing with secretaries, coupled with her own secretarial training and experience, make her an ideal person to advise others on most aspects of secretarial work. She has three children, all students, and runs her business from home in North-west London.

SERIES EDITORS: Stephen Coote and Bryan Loughrey

Secretarial Skills

Gail Cornish,
Charlotte Coudrille
and Joan Lipkin-Edwards

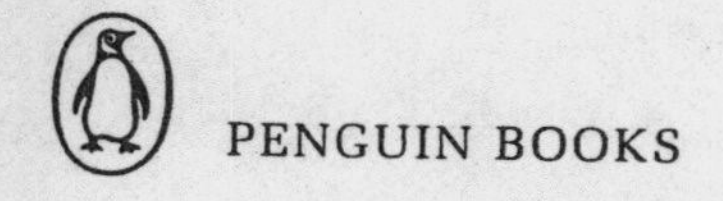

PENGUIN BOOKS

Published by the Penguin Group
27 Wrights Lane, London W8 5TZ, England
Viking Penguin Inc., 40 West 23rd Street, New York, New York 10010, USA
Penguin Books Australia Ltd, Ringwood, Victoria, Australia
Penguin Books Canada Ltd, 2801 John Street, Markham, Ontario, Canada L3R 1B4
Penguin Books (NZ) Ltd, 182–190 Wairau Road, Auckland 10, New Zealand

Penguin Books Ltd, Registered Offices: Harmondsworth, Middlesex, England

First published 1988

Typeset, printed and bound in Great Britain by
Hazell Watson & Viney Limited.
Member of the BPCC Group.
Aylesbury, Bucks
Typeset in Linotron Melior

Contents

Preface

This book is intended as an encouragement – an encouragement to all who, having attained shorthand and audio typing skills, are ready to expand their job into a fascinating career. It is assumed that those who read it will already have the basic secretarial skills of shorthand, typing, audio; nevertheless there is a detailed section on office machinery of all types, because a thorough working knowledge of modern office technology is important to today's career secretary.

This is not a handbook of advice to the senior secretary, nor is it an absolute authority on what must and must not be done in an office situation. Rather, it is an explanation of what being a secretary actually *is*, and an analysis of how to become one.

Much of it will be familiar to some readers, and some aspects will seem very elementary; but this book is aimed at a wide market, so it has been deemed necessary to treat the subject in depth.

The book is divided into two parts; the first deals with the actual business of *being* a secretary day by day; the second gives detailed descriptions of all types of office machinery and new (at the time of writing) technology, as well as some of the basic technology which has been in use for years; also some of the more common technical office procedures such as postal systems and so on.

Acknowledgements

Acknowledgements are gratefully due to Wendy Harris for her invaluable contribution to Chapter 6, Keeping the Accounts.

Also to Dr Stephen Coote for his unfailing patience and support during the tough bits, and for his belief in this book; and to Geoffrey Smith for all his help.

Last but not least, to Pitmans Secretarial College, The Association of Legal Secretaries, The Association of Medical Secretaries, Practice Administrators and Receptionists, British Telecom, The Post Office, The British Tourist Authority, Unique Freelance Secretaries, and many others too numerous to mention, all of whom made untold contributions in terms of giving information and help freely and at considerable length.

1 Being a Secretary

1 *The Secretary – Fallacies and Facts*

Do you know what a secretary is? Well, of course you do. She's that lady who sits behind the typewriter all day with plugs in her ears; she probably does shorthand or speedwriting and, with luck, can read it back; she does the filing and makes coffee; in cartoons she is either a dried-up, spinsterish old dragon in pointed specs, or nubile and sitting on the boss's knee; and by the twenty-first century she will be obsolete, all her functions having been taken over by superior technology.

Since you have got as far as picking up and opening this book we shall assume that you don't believe all of these fallacies, though you may have a sneaking suspicion that some of them are half true. But whether they are only half true at best or totally fallacious at worst, what then exactly *is* a secretary, as opposed to an audio or shorthand typist? If she is not to be obsolete by the twenty-first century there is obviously more to her than merely typing and making coffee; why is she not, therefore, a personal assistant? And, whatever may be the answers to these questions, is it worth your while trying to follow her into her career?

'Career?' we hear you ask. Surely we mean 'job'? For too long the role of the secretary has been considered as just a job, a filler-in for a girl before she finds a husband, or a sure way of earning a reasonable salary for the girl who was not too bright at school. (The word 'girl' is used advisedly – not that we think men incapable of being good secretaries, but secretarial work still tends, in this anti-sexist world, to be primarily a female preserve – and so, for ease of reading and perhaps also for elegance of expression, we shall refer to the secretary as female and the employer, generally, as male.)

A secretary is, or should be, a fully qualified professional woman in a career with promotional possibilities similar to any other. There are limitations, certainly, as there are in most professions, apart from the limitations imposed by her own capabilities, desires, ambitions or way of life. In one respect, however, the secretarial profession is unique in having no limitations whatsoever.

What are you interested in? What aspect of life or the world excites you? In which field could you most involve yourself? Answer any, and being a secretary can get you in.

Fashion? Cosmetics and fashion firms, fashion magazines, designers, need good secretaries.

Music? Opera houses, recording companies, orchestras, musical journals, managers, agents, all need good secretaries.

Drama? Theatre managements, theatrical schools, some actors, writers, impresarios, all need good secretaries.

Medicine? Doctors, hospitals, medical schools, clinics, all need good secretaries.

Estate agents, bankers, stockbrokers, lawyers, charities, architects, commercial business – the list is endless, but all of them, at some time or another, in spite of all modern technology, need a good secretary.

The essence lies in the word 'good', of course, which is really where this book comes in. Being a secretary is by turns fun, interesting, tedious, mundane, fascinating, exasperating, time-consuming and often chaotic – a bit like life, in fact. To be a good secretary you will need to be well grounded in the basic skills of shorthand and typing, and to have a fairly wide knowledge of office technology; you will also need tact, organizing ability, patience, loyalty and, above all, to *care*.

Given that you are, indeed, such a paragon, it is now up to you to choose. The ability to do shorthand and typing and to shove bits of paper into the correct folders will earn you a living – but there is a lot more to secretarial life than that. To be a secretary need not, and should not, mean being chained behind a typewriter bashing out lists or invoices for years on end. Never believe that 'this is it': 'this' being a beige room with a grey metal desk, looming filing cabinets and grimy windows: with a battered, cantankerous vending machine churning out drinks as grey as the desktop; with an ever-present Mr Foggit (Buying Clerk for forty-five years) trundling fussily to and fro in his stained suit, patting his single strand of hair and making you re-type an invoice for the tenth time because it isn't laid out *quite* as he likes it.

None of this is what being a secretary is about, and it is up to you to make the change.

Having changed, don't expect it to be all glitter and no filing. Even a very senior secretary or personal assistant has groundwork to do, which must always be done properly and will bore you to death if you let it; but to be a secretary is to have an open door to the world. The more complete your skills, the wider open stands that door.

2 How the World Sees You – Job Applications, Interviews

The Application

Now that you have decided to ditch Mr Foggit and try for better things, it is important to give prospective employers a good impression of yourself; and the first inkling they will have of your personality is from your application.

Whether or not you are seriously in the job market, it is as well to have a curriculum vitae (CV) prepared, from which all relevant details about you and your job experience can be assimilated quickly. It should be typed, of course; having done it, make some copies to keep for future reference. It is surprising how difficult it is to remember precisely when you changed one job for another when you are sitting in a reception area filling out an application form. You may find that, interestingly, you have apparently managed to be doing two jobs at once at opposite ends of the country!

A CV is an important document and should be done properly. It must be a factual summary of your background, education and work experience, not a woolly 'story of your life'. Keep it concise, in a formal style, without whingeing phrases such as 'I did not find that my hard work was appreciated' or 'I was victimized and sexually harassed by my boss.' In fact, leave out all the 'I's' and the little stories, and just stick to the facts, giving brief information about your responsibilities, salary, the nature of the firm's activities, etc. Try to convey an impression of efficiency so that *your* CV is good enough to make *you* the one they call for interview.

The following is the sort of CV you could use, although there are no hard-and-fast rules. Just be sure not to have any typing or spelling errors in it!

The details of your education need only encompass the secondary

CURRICULUM VITAE

PERSONAL DETAILS

NAME	Mary Jane FLOWER
ADDRESS	The Garden House, 19 York Road, London SW3 9TG
TELEPHONE	356 2198
NATIONALITY	British
DATE OF BIRTH	28th June 1960
STATUS	Single

EDUCATION

1971-1976	Bloggs Comprehensive School, Bloggstown, Middlesex. GCE Passes: French, Mathematics, English, History, CSE Passes: Art, Geography, Biology
1968-1971	Inspiration College of Secretaries, London Pitman's Shorthand - 100 wpm Typing - 60 wpm Shorthand-typing RSA stage II Current speeds are: Shorthand 130 wpm, Typing 75 wpm

EMPLOYMENT

Sep 1976-Apr 1977	Noughts & Crosses, Ltd, Advertising Agents, 99 Hill Street, London WC14
Position	Receptionist/Typist
Duties	Reception duties, typing lists, some client and production involvement.
Salary	£1,294
June 1977-July 1980	Small and Large Publicity Ltd, 1,100 Kings Road, Smalltown,
Position	Secretary to Chief Account Executive
Duties	Joined as a Typist to four account executives, progressed to assistant shorthand typist to Production Manager, and private secretary to Senior Account Executive, handling all private correspondence as well as having some responsibility for certain client accounts.

The customary presentation of a CV looks something like this school years, and although you do not need to stress your weak points (no need to *say* that you failed three times to pass O-level French) you should not over emphasize your strong ones. There's no harm in putting in your exam grades if you got good ones. 'First prize in mathematics every year for seven years; offered Head Teacher's job after being Head Girl for one term' might stretch credulity a bit; they might ask you for proof, and you might be expected to live up to the imaginary you. If you weren't one of the high-fliers at school this need not preclude you from having a brilliant secretarial career. Some of the best people did appallingly at school – Winston Churchill, for one – so don't be ashamed if you only scraped through with the minimum of CSE passes – you're probably in good company!

Apart from the obvious point of telling the truth, you should try to balance your CV so that there aren't glaring time gaps. If there is a short period when you had a slightly erratic time job-wise and you would rather not put it in writing, you can massage the dates a little without actually lying; otherwise, if you just leave a gap, potential employers might assume you've been in prison, or worse. 'A break while looking after young children' is fine, for example, on the CV of a woman going back to work after her family have started school.

Since we have just mentioned small children, it is appropriate to mention here that in all fairness to a potential employer you should also admit if you have any demanding dependants – aged relatives, young children or time-consuming pets – who may affect your ability to do overtime, or your overall commitment to the job. It is in fairness to you as well; it would be unrealistic to imagine that you could cope with the job of a director's secretary while hopefully relying on a neighbour to collect your toddler from playschool and give him tea, even if the salary offered is irresistible.

Lastly, give a brief list of your hobbies or interests, whether these be listening to records and knitting or abseiling down the Old Man of Hoy – they will give a potential employer a further insight into your character. (More to the point, if one of your interests was the latter, your employer might well have reservations about your being able to present yourself on time and in one piece every Monday morning – on the other hand, he might be inclined to join you!)

Remember to forewarn your referees *before* you have to ask them for a reference. It is unlikely that they will mind you using their names, unless you really have been a black sheep, but it's simple politeness to give them prior notice. It is as well to have more than one referee if possible; failing a previous employer, ask your family doctor, your solicitor, or someone who is in a profession who knows you well.

It is sometimes considered better if a photograph accompanies the CV – certain agencies may ask for one. Try a small photograph, but one step up from those dispensed by machines on railway stations – the 'startled fawn' look is not very appealing in a secretary!

If you are applying to an agency, replying to an advertisement, or even cold-calling (sending your CV on the off-chance that there might be something for you), you should send a covering letter. A typed letter is fine (you are *meant* to know how to type after all), but many firms prefer hand-written letters of application because handwriting is often a very good indication of character. Whichever you decide to do, the letter should be clear and concise, but not cold. 'Dear Sir, Please find enclosed my curriculum vitae which I hope will be of interest, Yours faithfully,' won't do. Try to catch their eye with a bit about why you think *you* would be just the perfect person to work for them, but don't go on for paragraphs, and don't put your CV in letter form. It will look like pages of close-typed chat, which is terribly off-putting for busy people. Keep your letter to one page and preferably three shortish paragraphs, and let the CV do the rest.

Here are a couple of examples:

> Dear Sir,
> In reply to your advertisement in Monday's edition of 'The Times' (June 4th), I have pleasure in enclosing my curriculum vitae for your attention.
>
> Although I have not had experience of working in the field in which your company is engaged, it is one which has always interested me. I am very happy in my present job but, having worked here for nearly two years, I feel it is time I broadened my experience and took on greater responsibility.
>
> I look forward to hearing from you at your convenience, and hope my curriculum vitae will be of interest.
>
> Yours faithfully,

Dear Sir,

I saw your advertisement in the 'Times' for a secretary and would like to apply for the position.

I enclose my curriculum vitae which I hope will interest you, and would be very pleased to hear from you with a view to making an appointment for an interview. I can make myself available at your convenience, but should be grateful if you would kindly avoid telephoning me at my office before 4.00 p.m.

I look forward to hearing from you.

Yours truly,

It seems marginally more friendly to put 'Yours truly' than 'Yours faithfully', if you are addressing a potential employer, even though you have started with 'Dear Sir'. Every secretary knows that 'Dear Mr . . .' and 'Yours sincerely' go together, while a letter starting 'Dear Sir' should end with 'Yours faithfully'; but a lot of employers do not; in any case, nowadays 'Yours truly' is a good compromise for 'Yours faithfully' and under certain circumstances sounds slightly less formal.

Don't worry about the phrase 'at your convenience', despite all the old jokes. There really is no other concise way of putting it, and business people take it as it is meant – one of the many classic phrases in business correspondence. Besides, that may well be the only place where your prospective employer can find a bit of peace and quiet to read his correspondence!

The Interview

You will be nervous! That is the first thing to remember, along with the fact that all those other cool, confident-looking applicants are like cats on a hot roof, too.

What you wear has a great effect on how you feel, of course, and may help or hinder your nerves as well. If you can choose something that is comfortable, that reflects your own style while also being suitable for the job at interview, so much the better. It is not our intention to make you change your style of dressing or to give a dissertation on fashion advice but, if you are not suitably dressed at an interview, you won't get past the reception desk, let alone get the job. Jeans are almost never suitable for an office, however well you know the firm and the people, although trousers are often all right. You must use common sense, of course. If you are trying to get the Girl Friday post in a company producing pop records, you will probably not be a howling success in a stiff little grey two-piece with a starched white collar. Conversely, you won't go down a bundle with the chairman of an old-established wine merchant's wearing your hair in a purple Mohican and safety pins in your nose.

Seriously, if you wear something comfortable and smart and, most importantly, something you feel good in, it will go a long way towards calming your jitters. You don't have to look like a fashion plate, and what you wear doesn't have to be brand new, but first visual impressions are important, so it's worth trying to look nice. You will feel more competent and efficient if your hair, nails and clothes are in order so that you look neat, well turned out and well groomed. (It is to be hoped that your desk, too, would reflect the state of orderliness in which you work – a point which a future employer might think was mirrored in the way you dress.)

A good speaking voice is a *must*; well modulated, unrushed, polite and self-assured, neither too bumptious nor too grovelling. You could make a tape recording of yourself, though this is often a terrible shock to the ego when it is played back. Try to cultivate a good voice for general use as well as for job applications, although we should say at once that this does not mean flattening out your regional accent until you sound like a speech therapist's nightmare.

Depending on the kind of job you are going after, you may go straight in to see the boss, but more probably you will meet the Personnel Officer first; if you go to an agency, you will be interviewed by one of their recruitment personnel, in which case you will almost certainly be asked to take a test involving a short piece dictated to your shorthand or speedwriting for you to transcribe back.

The interviewer will have seen from your CV what you say your speeds are and will try to dictate at approximately that speed; they may speak a bit faster just to see how you go, but if you say you take shorthand at 80 wpm, they are unlikely to dictate at 120 wpm. They are not masters of torture who *want* you to fail the interview – they are ordinary human beings looking for someone to fit their bill. They will know you are a bit nervous, that your hand may be shaking or the pencil slipping through sweaty fingers, so don't panic. Take a deep breath, pretend that you have been working here for years, and force yourself to concentrate.

Before going to type it back, ask a few sensible questions of the person giving the dictation: how do they like their name and title displayed? Do they like indented paragraphs? Is there a reference you should use? Are there any extra copies to be made? Then go and face that monstrous, unfamiliar typewriter which squats in some seldom-used corner, and which all the other self-respecting secretaries in the company refuse to touch.

Typewriters can be temperamental beasts at the best of times; even if you are presented with a model that is familiar to you, it will have its own little quirks and oddities; the touch will feel different and so on, so don't rush at it. 'Time is seldom wasted in reconnaissance,' a famous general once said, and this is certainly true where typewriters are concerned. Take a few seconds to find out about the machine, set tabs and margins and clear any previous ones; check that it is not set to type stencils! When you begin, type fairly slowly with a good, steady rhythm, even if you know you can type a lot faster. It will only take a couple of lines before you pick up speed, but if you start by trying to type as if the hounds of hell were after you, the result may be disastrous.

On the subject of disasters, it is a good idea to arm yourself with your own little supply of disaster averters: some correction papers, a bottle of correction fluid and even a typing rubber (some machines still use fabric ribbon), as well as a couple of shorthand pencils or pens, and maybe your own shorthand pad. It does nothing for one's self-confidence to have to search surreptitiously through a strange desk for something to correct a mistake, being covertly watched the while by a couple of efficient paragons who are typing at incredible speed with never a falter. Eventually, horror of horrors, you actually have to ask one of them for a piece of Tippex . . . and she takes ages to find it for you because, naturally, *she* hardly ever uses it!

Ask questions at the interview; don't leave it all to the interviewer. If you are applying for a job in a public company, it's not a bad idea to do a little homework a few days beforehand by looking at a copy of the *Financial Times* or seeking out the business pages of one of the other serious dailies. While you don't have to become a mastermind on the subject, some boning up will help you to ask a couple of intelligent-sounding questions. Although you will need to know about holidays, lunch-hours and so on, don't *just* limit your questions to 'How much free time do I get?' or 'What are the perks, apart from the salary?' It will sound as if you are only going in for what you can get out of it. Ask how many people there are in the firm, or in the office or the section in which you will work; what sort of work you will be expected to handle, will the boss want help with his personal affairs, club memberships, lunches; whether he uses shorthand or audio (or neither); are there any pension or health-insurance schemes assisted or paid for by the company. If you have a holiday already booked, you should mention this – most firms are quite understanding about the situation – and find out whether you will be expected to stagger holidays and lunch-hours with other members of the staff, or whether you are expected to work late – sometimes, often, never.

Discuss the salary in a matter-of-fact manner. You will probably know from the advertisement roughly what they intend to pay; if you ask a lot more, you will automatically disqualify yourself from the job, but if you mention that you had thought of just a little higher (say £500 up per annum, or possibly £1000 if you are in the £10 000+ range), you may well succeed if they have decided that, on all other counts, they would like to take you on. Of course, it may be that the Personnel Department is responsible for deciding salaries, or there may be a scale from which the employer cannot deviate at that particular level of employment for fear of causing uproar and discontent elsewhere in the firm. Here is where you have to make up your mind: choosing between less money and more fun, perhaps; or better money and possibly either more boredom or more pressure in another firm. Some of the best-paying firms are the ones where the work can be fairly monotonous (you have to be paid to be bored!), and most of the really fun jobs, like the music and record business, tend to pay rather less than average. Weigh up just how important money is to you. If you have a mortgage to pay, almost certainly you will have to cover a certain amount each month, but could you possibly manage on less, for the sake of enjoying the job more if it seems perfect in all other respects? Businesses frequently offer some indirect inducement as well as the salary.

Luncheon vouchers. Only the first 15p per day of a luncheon voucher is tax-free. This is a hangover from the days when they were first introduced, and three shillings a day bought an adequate lunch for an office worker. Most firms give a good deal more nowadays, and the company buys the vouchers at a higher cost than the face value of the vouchers to provide a profit for Luncheon Vouchers Ltd, or whoever else supplies the vouchers. They are a useful 'perk' but usually do not make or break the choice of a job.

BUPA/PPP More likely to affect your choice of a job could be whether private health insurance is offered. Firms which offer it usually have a condition, such as requiring staff to have been with the firm for a year or more before they can enjoy such a benefit.

Pensions and pension schemes. May not seem worth inquiring about when you are young, but as you grow older you begin to be more and more interested in the provision for a pension and whether your firm has a well-organized pension scheme. There are Government regulations regarding pension arrangements for employees, and you would do well to contact the Department of Health and Social Security (DHSS) and ask for their leaflets on the subject. You should, of course, discover before you take a job how well you are protected and whether, by changing jobs, you are likely to lose benefit overall.

Insurance policies. Some firms have indemnity policies for their staff, meaning that once they have checked their employees' references they insure their loyalty (that is, their financial honesty) with an insurance scheme known as 'fidelity bonding'. This sort of insurance usually applies where employees may be handling money and where possible losses can be ascertained for purposes of insurance. It is also obligatory for companies to have public liability insurance and employers' liability insurance, to protect both employees and visitors to their premises from potential loss owing to accidental damage to their persons or property.

Shorthand and Typing: Rusty or Speedy?

Before we close our discussion of the interview itself, we should touch on this nerve-racking subject. Unless you are fresh out of college or have recently taken a shorthand/typing test, you may not be quite sure what your speeds are – or even, if you are returning to work after a lengthy gap, whether you have any speeds at all!

It is possible that your shorthand may have lost some of its cunning; that is, it may become rusty through lack of use (like your brain at times, perhaps?), either because you have been in a job where you composed all your own letters or because you have been looking after children and not 'working' (joke!) at all. It is a fallacy that shorthand is going out of fashion now – there are still many employers who like someone to be able to take down their pearls of wisdom as they occur and who detest using a dictating machine which makes them feel like a machine, too.

Your typing probably won't suffer too much if it goes through a period of disuse. Generally, typing speed never drops below what it was when you finished your training; so if you left college with shorthand and typing of 100 and 50 wpm, your shorthand might have lost speed considerably (perhaps becoming so snail-like that you could type faster); but your typing, even with very little practice, will probably not be below 50, and it will speed up again quite quickly to what it was when you were working full tilt; and it might become even faster with electronic typewriters and word processors.

The news on radio is splendid for brushing up rusty shorthand. It is also a good move to buy yourself a shorthand book or magazine; that way you can update yourself on the correct outlines.

With a little effort you can check your speeds yourself at home. To test your shorthand, you will need a blank cassette, a tape recorder with a microphone, and a stop-watch or a watch with a second hand. The sample letter below is a fair guide:

Dear Mr. Brown,
This is to let you know that Mr. Green is away from the office this week and [¼] I am therefore keeping your letter of October 2nd (which only arrived today) until his return next Monday.

Meanwhile, I [½] confirm that the date for your meeting with the North of England sales force has been finalised for November 14th [¾] and I have made arrangements for the Conference Room in our Birmingham offices to be made available to you on [1] that day. There will be facilities for mid-morning coffee, and a buffet lunch in the Directors' dining room for [1¼] twenty-five people. Please let me know if these arrangements are satisfactory.

Unfortunately, Mr. Black will not be able to [1½] attend your meeting as he will be in the United States during the month of November, but I understand that [1¾] he has now approved the sales figures which you mention in your letter and as soon as the final draft [2] has been typed I will arrange for a copy to be sent to you. I am also sending you point [2¼] of sale and other promotional material on the new project which may be relevant to your sales meeting.

Yours sincerely, [2½]

As you see, it has been marked out in groups of twenty words for each quarter-minute, which would give you two and a half minutes at 80 wpm. If you are trying for 100 wpm you would, of course, need to divide the letter into twenty-five words per quarter-minute (the sample will give you two minutes at 100 wpm). Keeping an eye on the stop-watch, dictate into the recorder at the speed you require, remembering not to dictate punctuation marks; then play it back and take it down in shorthand.

Typing speed is worked out by the number of strokes per line, including punctuation and spaces. Choose a piece of prose about 400 words long (because you will need to work up a sustained speed to gain a true picture of your actual typing speed), and count the number of strokes, noting the totals, cumulatively, in the right-hand margin. Then type for five minutes without correcting mistakes. At the end of five minutes, count the number of strokes (including an unfinished line if there is one) that you have typed. Divide this total by five to give the number of 'standard' words (a 'standard' word being taken as five strokes), and then divide this new total by the number of minutes taken. The result will be your typing speed per minute. If you have made any mistakes, deduct a point for each one, thus reducing your speed accordingly. It takes about five seconds to correct one single letter – six mistakes in a piece, and you have lost half a minute – so concentrate on accuracy, if necessary slowing yourself down at first . . . you're not trying to beat the world speed record, after all.

Apart from reviving shorthand and typing skills, your basic office sense, once acquired, does not go away with the passing of the years; in fact, it becomes in distinctly greater demand when so many people in the secretarial marketplace today are considered inefficient by employers. There are refresher courses for secretaries, and sometimes the school or training college where you learnt your skills may re-train you free of charge, or at a greatly reduced rate.

Some secretarial agencies specialize in finding work for 'returners' (there are not many of these agencies, but they are worth locating), and will advise you on your chances, perhaps finding you temporary work while your children are of school age so that you can have time off in the holidays for haircuts, new shoes, outings, etc.

It is rare indeed for employers to complain at all about someone returning to work, and seldom just on the grounds of lost speed; sometimes they will demand fast typing and someone totally in practice, but very often a person who is conscientious and who types accurately, if rather more slowly, is preferred to a fast, inaccurate typist who makes constant mistakes. It is assumed that nobody is perfect; but an older secretary returning to work is usually closer to perfection, particularly as regards application and dedication to the job in hand.

To sum up, brush up your skills if you feel you are really out of practice, take a deep breath and re-launch yourself on to the secretarial market.

As a final corollary to this chapter: once your potential employer has made his decision in your favour, it is worth noting the sort of contract you could expect to receive, and what you should expect to find contained therein when you read through it.

Contracts and Rights

It is more reassuring to have a letter confirming your engagement from your employer, but anyway within the first three months of your employment you should be given a contract or at least a statement of the terms of your employment. This should set out the hours, rate of pay, time off, holidays, etc. You are also entitled to an itemized pay-statement and, if you are in a one-girl office and yourself responsible for the PAYE, you must make sure that your own national insurance contributions and tax are paid for you, via the firm.

After one month's continuous employment you are entitled to:

a minimum period of notice (you can be sacked at a minute's notice till then!)

pay during suspension on medical grounds

After two years' continuous employment (or one year if you started before 1 June 1985), you:

cannot be dismissed unfairly

cannot be dismissed for pregnancy

are entitled to maternity pay, time off and the right to return afterwards to the job

are entitled to redundancy pay

It is against the law to discriminate against anyone on grounds of their sex or their race.

There are safeguards for your holiday pay and any back pay in the case of an employer's insolvency.

There are reference books for employers (Croners) which contain all sorts of very useful information about employment, and give employees' rights in greater detail. The DHSS also issue various booklets to cover almost all eventualities; it could be useful for you to get one or more of them. Ring your local DHSS office for the list of titles, or go to your local library.

3 *Love Me, Love My Systems – Organizing Your Office*

So you got the job – Hooray! Now all you have to do is keep it.

Running an office is very like running a home; if you have never done either then you should know, first of all, that there are few hard-and-fast rules but several good stand-by hints that make life smoother.

It can take some time, and quite a lot of experience, to establish systems which work in your particular office. Many you learn from job to job, and some are taught as part of secretarial training. It is essential not to assume that *all* the systems already in existence in a new office are inadequate. In the new office there may be different ways in use for handling certain situations – a post book, say, or a petty cash system – which seems unusual to you. To start with, let it carry on and use the system yourself for a while. If after some time you find that it doesn't work as well as one you have used previously, you can then bring in the innovation, provided it doesn't cause a constitutional crisis.

If it appears to upset one or two people, try and discuss with them their reasons for preferring the old system; it may be that they know something you don't – perhaps the reason the last person was sacked was for trying to change the very same system! Of course this is unusual, but it is best to move slowly unless you are absolutely sure that your system is better, or you are starting a new office from scratch.

Starting on a general note, the first point to remember is not to let yourself run out of things, especially things you use only occasionally. You can bet that the one occasion you haven't bothered to renew whatever-it-is will be the very time you or your boss needs it desperately – *now*! Make a weekly check on everything: bond and bank paper (that is, top and carbon copy) in relevant sizes, usually

A4 and A5 for everyday office correspondence; matching envelopes and others of different weights, colours and sizes as necessary; air-mail stationery; pencils, ballpens, marker pens, fibre-tips; staples, paperclips, sticky labels, carbon paper, typewriter ribbons and correcting ribbons if your typewriter is a self-corrector; word processor disks, daisywheels, print-out tapes; anything peculiar to your job or company, like petty cash slips, invoice forms, sales order forms, personal detail sheets if you work in Personnel, and so on.

Check your boss's desk once a week, too. Make sure he has a stock of clean blotting paper, sharpened pencils, ballpens that work, fresh notepads, telephone jotters or whatever he uses to doodle on.

Keep a stock of shoe polish – black and brown should be enough unless your boss wears fancy colours – and suitable brushes, as well as a selection of buttons for suits and shirts, needles, and thread in one or two basic colours. It has been known for a secretary to do a lightning zip-repair job while her boss, clad in little more than his dignity, crouched behind his desk – so it might be worth keeping a spare trouser-zip or two as well.

You may have to keep a stock of drink and cigarettes for your boss, which must be checked regularly; depending upon the kind of office it is, don't be surprised if you need furniture polish, or even silver polish. Don't forget stocks of coffee, tea, sugar, dried milk powder, headache pills or other minor first-aid treatments.

On the subject of first aid, if you are in a large company it is likely that somebody will have done a St John's Ambulance first-aid course and will be in charge of the company first-aid box. Nevertheless, for everyday woes it is useful to keep some plasters and antiseptic cream somewhere alongside the aspirin and indigestion tablets (see also p. 42, Chapter 4, Just Me and My Shadow).

Make sure you never leave your office without a notebook and pencil(s) in your hand, or in your bag. It often happens that the boss will think of something as you are going down in the lift together, and the good secretary will make a note then and there, typing it back later. It is also useful to keep spare correction fluid (Tippex or Liquid Paper) on hand just in case, for some reason, you should have to work in a strange office. Some secretaries also like to keep a small dictionary with them.

Whether your office is small or large, don't be untidy. Piles of old trade journals on windowsills, files teetering on top of cabinets, typewriter uncovered (it will need servicing more often if you don't look after it), pencils, paperclips and staples in a jumble in the drawers, all make life impossible for the cleaners (who will probably just give up in the end) and defeat any attempts by you at efficiency, quite apart from encouraging the curious to take a peek into things that shouldn't concern them. Part of the word 'secretary' is made up of the word 'secret' – in other words someone who keeps secrets, or secretes things away from prying eyes. Which brings us to an important – if unpopular – subject.

Filing

Everyone's pet bugbear, but it has got to be done and is much less awful if you do it every day. Your files should be up to date and in a good system, which does *not* mean merely alphabetical.

Filing systems as such differ from firm to firm. If yours is a firm dealing largely in dates (as in calendar, not palm tree), a travel agency, for example, it will probably be best to have the filing in date order. If you are expecting clients to ring in or write frequently, you must be able to find their files quickly, and then perhaps an alphabetical system will be easier – everyone knows their own name, even if they forget the date they are going on holiday, or their reference number which you have asked them to 'quote in all correspondence'.

Numerical filing systems are normally used for enormous, indeterminate filing problems like Social Security departments and other governmental or civil service divisions, where the number/letter codes can be infinitely adapted – as you will have noticed if you have ever looked at the reference on a letter from one of these departments; it looks as though someone has grabbed a handful of tiles from a Scrabble board and chucked them indiscriminately at the paper, but the system probably makes sense to anyone who works there.

Many professional firms (accountants, solicitors and so on) file using an alphabetical system with numerical coding within the system, frequently updated by year, so that the current year's correspondence (court cases, affidavits, etc.,) can be easily to hand, the older files being kept in a central filing room or archives.

You can also arrange your filing system by location or subject (alphabetically within these headings, of course) if, for instance, your company has branch offices or important contacts in major cities around the country or elsewhere in the world. If your boss heads a sales team, you could file by each salesman's name, or his geographical patch, with the companies or products he is responsible for creating sections of their own in each case.

Introduce files for putting 'junk' literature in, if you think that the junk literature may come in handy one day, and index the filing so that you can actually *find* the stuff if ever you do need it. Giving such a file a title connected with its contents, rather than filing these things alphabetically, gives a better chance of finding them in two years' time: for instance, Computer Supplies – not Bloggs & Co. (computer supplies) – will mean that you can find Bloggs and Co., plus all the other supplies people, in the file. You will probably have forgotten Bloggs and Co.'s name after a few months, but you'll remember their business.

Whenever possible, systemize: have sheets for filling in details in tabulated form, rather than just trying to make a note of things. Each time you 'make a note' and attach it to a file you will probably access it in a different way; if you have columns for the items you are noting, it will be much easier to read later and your eye will go straight to the salient points.

Apart from general files, you will probably need a personal system for your boss and yourself, with details of his insurances (house, car, all risks, medical, school fees), his bank, his solicitor, dentist, doctor, (psychiatrist?!), tax, mortgage, credit cards, details of his salary, and maybe those of other people, too.

Whichever kind of basic main system you use, it is a good idea to keep at least one date system going – that is, thirty-one files labelled 1–31 – best kept in the filing drawer in your desk (assuming your desk has one). If there is no filing drawer, then do try and find a niche for this invaluable system. Anything to be brought forward for a certain date can be put into the relevant pocket (for example, papers for a meeting on the 15th of next month into pocket 15) and, provided you remember to check it daily, it is almost impossible to forget to give your boss everything he needs on that date. It is particularly useful for someone who travels a lot and will need a variety of different papers or files for his travels, which otherwise might be overlooked in the last-minute fluster. A casual aside – 'By the way, I shall want to take this with me to Buenos Aires' – tossed out in the middle of a mammoth dictating bout a month before his trip is horribly easy for both of you to forget; but filed into the date pocket of the last day you will see him before he leaves, it is there to be checked and verified with him. (*Don't* put it into the pocket for his actual departure date, because by the time you get to it he will already be gone!) Special documents for an important meeting, something you want to discuss with him tomorrow morning, a telephone message you have already given to him that is relevant to some event a week hence – anything, in fact, that will be needed in the near future but might slip through the memory net will be safely brought forward by using this system. It is, as we have said, invaluable and works infallibly with one proviso – DON'T FORGET TO LOOK IN IT!

Another date-based system which many employers like to use is the Day File of all correspondence from your office. In other words, an extra carbon copy is taken of everything you type except, perhaps, the most confidential items, and put into a ring binder in date order so that there is always a record easily to hand. It can be used as a sneaky memory-jogger to you, too. If there is some ambiguity about where to put the main file copy (perhaps there are two or more equally logical alternatives), you can make a small pencil note on the Day File copy telling you where you finally decided to put the main copy. This can be a life-saver when your boss suddenly requests 'the correspondence on such-and-such', and you know perfectly well that he wants *all* the relevant correspondence on the subject. Of course, if you have filed some of the other relevant correspondence in a different file and forgotten which one, then you're sunk – and the moral of that is: don't!

A new filing system is one of the greatest changes you can instigate and should be worked out in detail in advance. The best time actually to carry out the dirty deed is when your employer is safely away on a business trip so that, apart from taking his messages (and the million other things that crop up in his absence), you can get on uninterrupted. Once you have a clear idea of what you are doing, a new system can be functioning quite quickly; but make sure that your boss will be able to use it himself – it is *his* work you are filing away for posterity, after all.

As to the best kind of system in which to house your files, you will find this dealt with in greater detail in Chapter 27, Filing Systems, but nearly all are made to lock securely; you should be meticulous about doing this at night or if you are going to be out of the office for some time. You would be surprised at how much nosy people want to find out, especially if you are working for someone very senior.

So keep your files filed, properly tagged and in good condition. Replace torn and old folders, keep filing-tabs clean and readable, make sure the filing pockets are properly joined together, create a sister file for a current one that has become elephantine and unmanageable, *but* and it is a big *but – do not throw anything away*. Your filing system will need a spring-clean every year, and a major weeding session every two or three years, but even then be careful what you decide to consign to the shredder.

If you work for a large company, they will probably have a central archive where old files are stored or, more likely nowadays, a microfilm department (much less space-consuming). If, on the other hand, you are 'one girl/one boss', you may need to create your own archives. NEVER throw away anything that smacks even slightly of the law: leases, sales agreements, rental agreements, contracts, or any correspondence that makes reference to such things. Even if they are ten years old or more, they can still rear an ugly head when you least expect it. NEVER throw away cheque-book stubs or bank statements, or copy invoices – here again unexpected queries needing verification can pop up years after the event. To use a (hopefully) unlikely but dramatic example, if your boss were to die suddenly, his widow would need the cheque-book stubs and bank statements as proof of what accounts had or had not been paid, otherwise she would be lost. The friendliest family greengrocer, who has smilingly extended credit for years, will be round for his money like a bolt of lightning if he thinks he may have to wait six months until probate is granted. Likewise Harrod's Accounts Department.

Having made up your mind as to what you can safely dispose of (and if in doubt, don't), find some way of eliminating it completely. Remember the stories about schoolboys finding top-secret MoD material on municipal scrap-heaps? If your company has not got a shredder or disintegrator, the local library may be able to help. Failing that, take the whole lot home, separate it, rip it up and deposit it in separate batches amongst your vegetable peelings – the most hardened industrial spy would think twice about rootling around elbow-deep in rotting carrot peel. Do not just tear things in half and dump them in your wastepaper basket for the office cleaners to clear away.

Have baskets for things; not just IN and OUT, but for TODAY'S WORK, FILING, BOOKKEEPING and URGENT ATTENTION, and *keep looking through them*. Don't leave them to pile up with things which you may look at one day.

Address lists

It may seem absolutely elementary to talk about address books and putting addresses into them, but it is not unknown for a secretary to keep an address book with two addresses in it – her own and her employer's!

Have a good, hardback alphabetical book, or a card-index system, and keep it up to date. Don't rely on getting addresses out of the files – it is terribly time-consuming and inefficient, especially for anyone who might have to step into your shoes while you are away. Cross-reference your addresses:

Under 'B': Joe BLOGGS
(see Smith & Co.)

Under 'S': SMITH & CO.
3 Harbour Way,
Anytown.
(Joe Bloggs, Sales Manager)

If this seems unnecessary, remember that your boss will probably say, 'Letter to Joe Bloggs', or 'Write to Smith's'. If you have not cross-referenced, a temp may search for ages not knowing that Joe Bloggs works for Smith & Co. It is also possible that if you have only written to Joe Bloggs once, six months ago, even *your* exceptional secretarial memory might need a bit of help!

The pros and cons of a card-index box as opposed to an address book really boil down to your personal preference. A book is more portable, for the secretary who may spend much of her time out of her office, at conferences for example. The card-index system is more flexible, though, since (i) no matter how many names are added, you can keep it in strictly alphabetical order; (ii) because the cards are typed (or should be), everyone can read them easily; (iii) there is also enough space to make little notes if necessary; minor changes or additions can easily be done; in fact, a card can become quite cluttered with information without affecting the rest of the system; and (iv) finally, any card can, of course, be renewed when necessary, again without affecting the rest.

Computerization

It is possible that your office, having always used manual systems for recording index cards, books with numbers, cross-referencing, etc., is 'computerizing'. If you are totally unfamiliar with computer systems, DO NOT PANIC. Get cups of coffee (for everyone, as they are probably all feeling the same way) and start to learn what is required. Jobs often change with the introduction of computer systems, but the essence of what your firm does will not change, and your office still requires a good secretary to keep everything under control – including the boss, who may be the worst panicker of all!

Make sure that the computer installation people give you enough documentation on:

the way the system works

what it is supposed to do

how you are supposed to use it

Also be sure that you know:

how to make it work (getting it going in the morning, for example)

who to get hold of when it doesn't (they all break down, 'crash' and/or have their little foibles and off-days)

Do not hesitate to shout for help from the suppliers of the machine (the hardware) or the program (the software). Word processing is often just another software package on a computer and is therefore not exempt from the same problems which can beset all programs. If you have a 'dedicated' word processor, there is a better chance of fewer 'crashes' during operation, and therefore a better chance of an easier life for you if you do a lot of word processing. On the whole, word processing packages are more complicated to use if they are part of other programs run on a computer. A dedicated word processor is to be preferred if you are going to be using it mainly for that purpose, even if your firm has a computer system elsewhere in the organization. In fact, a PC (personal computer) *and* a word processor can be very useful for a small company. It is not often that they will share the same printer, as the word processor needs a 'letter quality' printer, probably with a daisywheel, or possibly a laser printer, whereas a computer needs fast print-out, better achieved with a cheaper method like a dot-matrix printer, whose quality is not so high (more on this in Chapter 23, Word Processors).

As the office secretary, you should be as thoroughly familiar with new technology as possible. Since it seems to change every day you are probably, regrettably, never going to be able to be completely up to date, but if you can go on a course occasionally, it will be of great benefit to you.

Whether or not your system is computerized, it is a good idea to have a list of the places where things are put, for example:

Index cards clients' names and addresses and line of business.

Inquiry forms ways of dealing with inquiries

Booking sheets for firm orders

Internal audit sheets

Stationery requisition forms pre-typed with all possible requirements, and space for some you didn't think of

and keep a note of the number of carbons, the colours of copies, to whom copies of what should be addressed, what happens to invoices, inquiries, bookings, orders, payments, post, etc., so that, when 'flu strikes, someone can come in and take over to some extent, thus saving your boss from being left high and dry. (If you think that he might appreciate you more if you make the system incomprehensible to anyone but you, think again. This is *not* the mark of a good secretary. Your replacement should be the best you can get, and should meet with a system that she can cope with as if it were her own. Only in that way will your boss be kept happy enough to reassure you, on your return, that had it not been for the efficient way you run the office, he and the temp could never have managed in your absence!)

Supplies

Everyone wants to get in on the act of supplying these days, particularly to computer users, and you need to weed out the quality from the rubbish, the reliable from the wholly unreliable, and the stable companies from those which are about to go out of business (they do it all the time).

It can be cheaper (and as good) to buy computer labels from one firm, continuous stationery from another, pre-printed invoices for computerized accounting systems from a third, and other printing and stationery from yet another. You will not find any shortage of willing salesmen at your door once they know you are interested; some of them may pester you, but it can't be helped and you don't have to do business with every salesman who telephones.

Their enthusiasm knows no bounds while they are trying to convince you that you should buy *their* piece of equipment; the problems start when the three-month guarantee period is over and your firm has paid for the new machine. Then it can be *so* hard to contact your salesman, especially if something goes wrong. Of course this is not always the case; but somehow, when the first flush of keenness is over and they have supplied you with most of the items which make up the one system or machine you are buying, it may really be quite hard work getting them to bring over the final pieces: the keyboard which has the extra amendment you asked for, or the spare diskettes – or even the instruction manual!

Naturally you should build up a suppliers' file so that you know who to approach when necessary, but, as it is not a constant requirement, just keeping a file with the relevant telephone numbers and latest price-lists is generally enough.

Keep a note of maintenance contracts on typewriters and other equipment and when they need renewing. You will probably be reminded by the contractor, and they should send someone once or twice a year (or more often) to give the machines a look over. Note when each machine is serviced, what goes wrong and how long it takes to get it put right. If you are dissatisfied with service of any sort, remember you have the option to go elsewhere, unless of course the maintenance contract is part of the rental price of the machine. Your firm may use a regular supplier; in this case, unless you can prove that they are grossly inefficient or hugely overcharging, it is better not to change, since the boss of the supplier may be a golfing friend of your own employer. *Always* move carefully when trying to make changes.

Messages

This, like address books, may seem an elementary subject to cover when discussing the duties of a senior secretary, but message-taking and giving can (again like address books) be done properly or lackadaisically, and there is a wealth of difference in the results.

When telephoning a message, always ask the message-taker to read it back. It is very easy for your abject apologies, for example, to get left out if the message-taker is not as precise as she might be. Names, too, can be muddled – even a quite straightforward name like 'Wills' has been known to be converted to Wells or Willis (and once, by some superhuman stretch of imagination on the part of the message-taker, 'Witts!') – so make sure they have got it right.

Don't delay in giving messages, even if you're very busy; preferably, give the message earlier rather than later, to allow time for a reply, should one be forthcoming. If you are asked to ring someone back, DO IT! It is maddening to have to wait, perhaps to finish a long, complex piece of typing or planning which cannot be completed until someone has returned your call.

When receiving messages, take them down clearly on a proper message pad, not on a scruffy piece of paper which will get lost. Ideally, you should type them out: your boss shouldn't have to struggle with your idiosyncratic handwriting – it's your job to struggle with *his*. Some secretaries like to keep a copy of all messages they take, and this is a good idea if you are working for more than one person. A hardback receipt book is best for this, with a piece of carbon to interleaf between two pages so that you can leave one copy on the desk of the would-be recipient and keep the other yourself until you are sure the message has been received. Even when you are sure that it has, don't throw away your copy. Draw a line through it and impale it on an office spike, where it should stay for a few days. You can have a weed-out every so often when the spike gets over-full but, to be on the safe side, keep these copy messages at least until the end of the week.

Another alternative is to have a shorthand pad chained to your desk on which you, and anyone else, can write messages. In this case of course, the messages are crossed out and kept until the shorthand book has been completely used, but the pad has to be chained to your desk to prevent 'anyone else' walking off with it; the snag about this method, of course, is that the messages are handwritten, so there is a greater chance of misreading a name or a telephone number.

Wall Charts and Pin-boards

On the whole, a pin-board is something to be avoided. It tends to get cluttered up with everybody's holiday postcards or ancient tatty lists, the purpose of which has long been forgotten.

The danger is that you *think*, if you pin that note up, you will remember to do something about it: but it becomes yet another grotty piece of paper, hardly noticeable until it is too late. If you do have a pin-board, be very strict with yourself and use it only for a few severely controlled and defined items: internal telephone lists, branch office address lists and so on. Do not use it as a memory-jogger – it will become a memory-clogger, however hard you try.

Yearly wall charts can be very useful, however, particularly if you have to keep track of several people, or if your boss does a lot of travelling. These are large , plasticized, coloured calendars on which you can stick different coloured strips or symbols (and there is a 'key' space so you don't forget what your colours and symbols mean!). If you organize it properly and keep it up to date, you will be able to see at a glance the dates when your boss will be away, or when the next management meeting is scheduled, or whatever other useful information of that kind you may use the chart for. Remember to order a new one well before the end of the year, as there is bound to be some overlap, and they sell like hot cakes.

Travel Information

There is more about this in Chapter 5, Organizing Your Boss, but since we are talking about systems there is one that should be mentioned if your boss travels abroad a great deal, particularly to the Middle or Far East, Australia, Africa or South America, behind the Iron Curtain or to North America. For most of these places your boss will need a visa; for the more exotic locations he will also need certain inoculations, against typhoid, cholera, yellow fever, malaria and so on. The inoculations are a real beast; they all require different quarantine times until they become fully effective, and they are effective for different time-spans so it is essential to have an efficient system for keeping track of all this otherwise you and your boss will be sunk.

Once again a large, alphabetical, hardback book, or a card-index system separate from your address system, should be kept. Under the relevant letter, keep notes on (i) country, (ii) inoculations and/or visa requirements, (iii) amount of money he took last time, (iv) length of last visit, (v) when his inoculation and/or visa is due to run out, etc. Then cross-reference information about the vaccines under the relevant letters, giving details about the quarantine time, length of efficacy, any side-effects (he may find himself in bed with a roaring fever for three days – it's best to warn him in advance!); under P for Passport, keep details of his passport, number, date of renewal; and under V for Visas, list all the visas he holds, dates of expiry and how difficult it may be to renew one, and a note of any friendly contact you have found in a relevant embassy who has smoothed the visa-obtaining path for you before. Friends in the right places are very important to the secretary (the 'right' places not always being 'high' places) – so important, indeed, that we have devoted a chapter to them in their own right; embassy folk don't figure very large in that chapter, but if you have made a friend in the visa department of an embassy, remember to keep a check on him. Embassy officials don't normally stay in their posts for longer than about two years, so make sure he puts you in touch with his replacement before he leaves.

You will, of course, devise your own systems, some of them pets which you take with you from job to job to assist you in your own personal efficiency, some of them adapted from existing systems you inherit; like cars or bicycles, they will work wonderfully and carry you for years as long as you keep them constantly oiled and serviced. In others words, don't neglect any system and then be surprised when it lets you down. A few minutes' attention for revising and up-dating when you have a spare moment is well worth it, to avoid days or even weeks of work trying to reconstitute the thing once you have let it fall into disuse.

A good system is a lovesome thing, so learn to love yours!

4 *Just Me and My Shadow – The One-Girl Office*

Before going on to discuss other aspects of office management, it is worth mentioning the situation where one girl runs an office consisting of either one man and his business, or a small team, and lacking the back-up offered by large companies of a central filing room, telephone exchange, post room, canteen staff, etc.

In the one-girl office everybody is busy doing what they have to do, and they are all dependent on you to see that the day-to-day running of the office is under control. You have to know where everything is, what time everyone will be back, take their messages, explain unexpected absences, make the coffee, lick the stamps, take down, type and post the letters, probably do the banking and type the invoices, and perhaps even write the cheques.

You will have command of the first-aid box (see Chapter 31, p. 173) and may even have taken the St John's Ambulance first-aid course so that you can resuscitate members of the office from terminal hangovers or nurse them through the agonies of a cut finger.

As a newcomer to a one-girl office, it can be awkward, especially when you discover things which are not to your liking (not, one hopes, the people!). If you have no experience of being a 'big fish in a small pond', tread carefully; it is surprisingly easy to offend people, especially when the new broom rushes in and sweeps cleaner than others are used to.

If things are unclear to you, ask and keep on asking until you have got things straight, otherwise you won't really be able to make your job what it should be.

Apart from the things mentioned above, there will be the 'housekeeping' matters which will also fall to you to deal with. For example, most offices nowadays have plants, and these will almost certainly be your province. Be careful with them, even if you know nothing about plants, or loathe them – they may be a present from the boss's wife to celebrate some anniversary.

If you have no idea how to look after them, describe them over the phone to a local florist, or ask a knowledgeable friend. Make a note of when each plant should be fed and watered (the same with the office cat, if there is one), re-potted or whatever is necessary, and keep the note handy for instant reference. Here is an instance where the dreaded pin-board can come in useful, it is an ideal place to keep lists or notes of this kind. In any case, don't let the plants (or the cat) die from neglect.

Find out how the boss likes his coffee, whether there is an electric percolator, filter-coffee maker, or merely a jar of instant: and, if one of the former, learn to use it. Don't ask him every time if he takes sugar; make a note until you can remember (the same applies to the other members of his team). Don't regard yourself as being above coffee-making just because you have reached a particular level; the best secretaries *have to* be willing and able to make coffee and lick stamps. Check, too, if the boss has a particular cup he likes, and make sure he gets it; and wash it up between uses (oh yes, washing up *is* part of your job, especially in a one-girl office!).

While on the subject of coffee, be ready and available to make coffee when important (or less important) clients are there, or arrive unexpectedly. When making coffee for several people, don't go round asking everyone whether they take milk and sugar. Take in a tray, with coffee in a jug, cups and saucers, milk in a jug, sugar in a bowl, spoons, and biscuits on a plate. This may seem like elementary advice, but if you normally hand your boss his coffee in a mug ready milked and sugared, you should remember that this is not quite the thing when he has visitors.

Before you took the job, you might have had an opportunity to speak to the outgoing secretary. Ideally, she will at least have left you some notes, a list perhaps, of the daily and weekly happenings and likely callers. Use it frequently. Check how the boss likes his telephone calls handled – 'Mr Jones's office', 'Extension such-and-such', 'Jones Incorporated' or whatever – and how he likes them dealt with in his absence. Create a telephone message system if one is not already in existence.

In a modern, high-tech office you may have a computer terminal on your desk connected to the boss's computer, with a diary facility on it. Check that both of you are to use it – but still confirm by memo, so that he doesn't miss an appointment you have made for him.

In a one-girl office you may actually be part of a large empire, so that, although you may feel in charge of everything, there is in fact an overriding system which you cannot change. In such a situation, when people from branches come to your office or when you go to meetings, seminars, etc., do not get involved in 'office politics'. Don't complain about your office, firm, organization in any way; nor about your boss; nor about anyone working for the firm. Anything said in such circumstances, which is a lapse in your loyalty, always gets straight back to where you don't want it.

If your job is in your boss's home, you may find yourself involved to some extent in the domestic side of life. The milkman may call to be paid, the children may come home from school unexpectedly, friends of your boss may call in (bosses don't always want to see their friends during business hours, so be discreet in case he wants to pretend to be out). The washing-machine man/gas man/plumber may call, and you can probably deal with them without pestering your boss. If you get on well together, it can be very pleasant to sit in the garden at lunchtime, and meet the boss's friends – at normal odds some, at least, may be eligible men!

Keep a sense of humour at all times – insults hurled round the office are seldom aimed at you personally, and are probably quickly regretted when the pressure that caused them is off.

5 *Organizing Your Boss*

The logical step, from talking about organizing yourself, is to talk about organizing your boss, but this is a very difficult subject to generalize on. Some bosses do not want to be organized; some hardly need to be; others are chaotic, impossible to control and very good at disorganizing *you*. Let's assume, though, that you work for an average person, neither too efficient nor too disorganized to afford you the chance to do a bit of tactful organizing in your own way.

The following gives a rough idea of how a secretary might set about it; but remember, these are only general comments. Each office is as different as its neighbour, contains different personalities with different demands, and has different running requirements, so do not look on this chapter as a *modus operandi* for your plan of campaign.

At the beginning of the day it is usually best if you arrive in the office before your boss – although some employers always like to beat their secretaries to it and seem to be prepared to come in at four in the morning if it will mean the girl arrives five minutes after them. However, we are assuming that you are working for Mr Average, so you will arrive before he does and have a chance to check over his office, make sure it's clean, that the wastepaper basket is empty, any dead flowers are replaced with fresh ones, dirty cups or glasses removed (office cleaners don't always do these things); also that the diary is open on the correct day, with *everything* he is doing that day marked in it (see Chapter 3, p. 31, on diaries). Also check that the calendar, if he keeps one, is open to the correct day, and that the clock is wound and telling the right time.

If he has meetings that day, or is seeing someone specifically, put on his desk any relevant files or papers (which you will have retrieved from your Date File system, because you do remember to check it every morning without fail, don't you?). Loose papers should be clipped together or slipped into a folder so that they don't fly about, perhaps with a note pinned to them, 'for Meeting with Bloggs', so he knows what they're about. (There are useful little sticky notepapers nowadays which come in different colours and sizes and have a strip of non-permanent glue at the top so that they can be stuck on to something and peeled off afterwards with no ill-effect.)

Some bosses like to open the mail themselves, but most are happy for you to do it and then to arrange it so that they're not bothered with circulars or anything they can read later when they have more time. Unless you know your boss and everything about him very well, you probably should not open anything marked 'Personal' or 'Private and Confidential' – in some offices there are subtle shades of meaning to these phrases: 'Private and Confidential' indicates that the secretary *can* open it but shouldn't leave it lying about. The desperation of a correspondent sending something he *really* wants no one but the recipient to see becomes apparent when an envelope is laden with the instructions 'Strictly Personal and Private To Be Opened By Addressee Only'! Anyway, on the better-safe-than-sorry principle, leave the 'Personal' and 'Private' letters for your boss's eyes only, but open everything else and READ IT. Part of your job as a secretary (as distinct from that of a shorthand typist) is to sift information. As you get to know your job better, you should be able to reply to many of his letters, simply passing the replies to him to sign, or possibly saving him even that effort; or précis a long report for him, giving him the salient points which need immediate action, leaving the bulk of the thing for him to wade through later.

Having decided what you can deal with, arrange the mail in order of priority, with the unopened letters on top. If there is something you know he *must* read, clip a small piece of coloured paper to it (or one of the sticky notes) to make it stand out from the rest, and put it near the top of the pile. Any letters you have answered on his behalf should be placed near the bottom with your reply clipped to the back, so that he can see what you have said.

Check that letters mentioning enclosures actually contain them (the commonest of all secretarial mistakes, this). If one is missing, having made sure it is not still hidden in the envelope, attach a note for your boss, for example 'cheque NOT enclosed', and make certain that he has registered the fact. One of you will have to get in touch with the sender immediately so that they can replace the enclosure without further delay.

Unless he simply hates it, have some coffee on the go, ready for him when he comes in; leave him in peace with his coffee and his post for twenty minutes or so, preferably with the telephone switched through to your office so that you can politely but firmly discourage any callers. Be like Cerberus guarding Hades with any visitors, first thing in the morning. Of course, if the Managing Director wanders in, there is little you can do; but colleagues drifting by for an idle chat, where five minutes can easily stretch to a couple of hours, should be greeted by a charming, but immovable dragon.

Once you feel he has had enough time to digest some of the information on his desk, ask him if he would like you to come in (in a tone of voice that expects the answer 'Yes'), and unless he specifically says, 'No', go in, armed with your shorthand pad, pencils, diary and anything else you feel to be important; in other words, beard him in his den before anyone else does. Tell the switchboard that you are going in to dictation, and ask her to take messages on all but the most vital calls – vital calls for *him*, by the way, not for you! (One point here, incidentally, on a small matter of etiquette: if you also have a cup of coffee to get you started in the morning, don't just march into his office with it. However well you know him, always ask if you may bring it with you. He will probably never say you may not, but you should maintain this little courtesy to him.)

Obviously you will not always be able to organize his morning like this – each day's itinerary varies considerably – but if you can try to get the main batch of dictation out of the way first thing, it is a great help, otherwise you may find yourself sitting about for the greater part of the day knowing there is a heap of mail waiting to be answered, which will be flung at you at a quarter to five with little chance of getting most of it out the same night.

Some bosses do fall into the bad habit of drifting about for the first couple of hours in the day chatting with colleagues, until it is time for a meeting when they will, naturally, be incommunicado for some time; then comes lunch, followed by another meeting, and the post doesn't even get thought about until late in the afternoon. How firm you are able to be about this depends on your boss's nature and your relationship with him; but for your own peace of mind and efficiency, it is worth trying to establish the habit of early-morning tête-à-têtes with him.

These tête-à-têtes are important because they give you a chance to talk about things other than the dictation – for instance, to co-ordinate your diaries. There may be appointments that he has made in your absence which you should know about, and there may be other items that you simply wish to remind him about, like birthdays or retirements, special requirements for a conference or an overseas trip. Or perhaps you simply want to fill him in on a bit of office gossip. Whatever the topics, these morning meetings may be the only time in the day when the two of you can have any time together, so preserve them whenever possible.

While on the subject of diaries, his should contain details of meetings he attends, people he sees, conferences he runs, trips he takes, any important birthdays or anniversaries he should remember; yours should contain all that, *and a whole lot more*. Anniversaries of any kind, for example, should not only be marked in your diary on the relevant day, but also in large (red?) letters a few days before, so that you can remind your boss in good time. Your diary should mark an important telephone call, tell you what a VIP guest was given to eat last time he visited, or warn you that an impending VIP has, say, an allergy or a religious denomination preventing him from eating certain kinds of food (a famous Jewish take-over king *was* served roast pork the first time he lunched with the directors of a newly acquired company!). Your diary should also contain dates of machine servicing, when a vital report or telex was sent, reminders of an extra person who should have been invited to a meeting (this would be in the Minutes of the meeting, of course, but by the time you need the information to hand the Minutes might have gone down to the archives). As such, your diary becomes a sort of office Bible – a lasting record of things accomplished – and it should therefore join the list of items you never throw away. Keep some convenient bookshelf, or corner in a cupboard, for old diaries – you will be surprised how often something crops up in later years which can be quickly checked by flipping through the diary of the year in question. Like the yearly wall chart, you should remember to order diaries for both your boss and yourself well before the end of the year. (*That* reminder should be in your diary, too!)

Another thing that should be in your diary – if your boss does a lot of travelling abroad – is a note, well before the date of a prospective trip, to check his passport, visas, inoculations, etc. This should remind you to look up your A–Z travel system described in Chapter 3, but even if you are sure you have all the up-to-date information there, it is worth getting hold of his passport, etc., for a final check-up. Also, of course, you should have mapped out his itinerary and ordered his tickets several weeks in advance, as well as having ordered foreign currency for him, for which you may need his passport. It is absolutely vital to do all this in plenty of time. If he does need a visa renewed (or even a new passport), remember that the wheels of Petty France and visa departments grind exceedingly slow, and it's no good shrieking at them in a panic two days before he leaves. If he is forgetful – nag!

When making travel arrangements for your boss, find out which class he wants to travel. He may be modest in his demands, not wishing to fling company money about, but if he has a long itinerary in terms of both time and world coverage, try and persuade him to go first class, or even VIP. It really does make a great difference to his comfort and convenience; and if the firm thinks he is good enough to represent it on such an important trip, it should be prepared to come up with the wherewithal to cushion him a little.

Following this train of thought, it may also be a good idea to book double rooms for him; and if he asks you to do so, don't leap to the obvious conclusion, even if there is an attractive lady from a rival firm travelling on the same route! Many modern hotels have single rooms so small you can barely swing a toothbrush in them, so he will appreciate the extra space a double room will afford, and the extra cost is often minimal.

Mapping out the itinerary for a long and complex overseas trip involving several different countries takes time and care, especially if your boss is not to return feeling like a wrung-out dishrag, dissatisfied with his own performance and thoroughly jet-lagged. First of all, get together with the travel agent (see Chapter 7 on your Best Friends) and work out the whole thing, with time losses or gains, the crossing of the International Dateline or the equator and what this will mean in terms of sleep schedules, the availability of suitable flights, hotel bookings to coincide with work schedules, and so on.

Once you have got the whole thing beautifully tied up, get together with the travel agent *again* when your boss suddenly remembers a vital conference in Buenos Aires on the 12th which must be squeezed in between the sales meeting in New York on the 10th and his appointment in San Francisco on the 16th. (Since the Americas are so huge, he will be crossing the Dateline once and the equator twice, which will muck up all the flight schedules; and while he can gain a couple of hours flying from New York to Buenos Aires, he will lose five from Buenos Aires to San Francisco – unless, of course, he is travelling between 29 April and 26 October, in which case he will lose only four hours because of US Daylight Saving Time – but then again, if he should land in Arizona on the way, he will lose five hours, because Arizona does not observe Daylight Saving Time, but he will gain one on entering San Francisco. All this still being dependent on the hope that (a) you can rearrange all the hotel bookings, (b) all the good hotels, and some of the bad ones, in Buenos Aires are not booked solid due to the conference, and (c) you can make any of the flights connect suitably . . . well, you begin to get the picture!)

If you and your friendly travel agent decide the whole thing has become impossible without your boss being consigned to a strait-jacket on his return, synchronize your stories and then go back to the office and tell him a lie. Say it is impossible for him to make such-and-such a connection without a ten-hour stopover, book him into the best hotel you can find near the airport so that he is forced, at the worst, to catch up on a day's rest, and let him chafe. In the end he will probably be grateful for it.

Something else he will probably thank you for, although initially you may have your head snapped off, is the occasional untimely interruption by you. If he has an appointment and is busy with a colleague, he may be a bit ratty when you pop your head round the door to remind him, but he'll be far rattier if you say nothing and he's late as a result.

Try not to lose track of him. This is easier said than done with some people who are as slippery as eels and disappear the minute your back is turned; but if you catch sight of him slithering out of the office, pin him down as to where he's going. It may turn out to be the Gents; but never mind – at least you know!

Giving some thought to the timing of things is another way for you to smooth his path through the business day. Most men nowadays have hair appointments (as opposed to a quick trip to the barber) and some even a manicure. Since hairdressers don't always work exactly to the minute, try to arrange the appointment on a day when he is not rushed off his feet and when his favourite stylist is available. At the very least, a hair appointment should be an occasion for your boss to unwind a little; nothing more inclines a person to high blood pressure and peptic ulcers than sitting, trapped and dishevelled, under the scissors watching the clock tick inexorably past the time of an important meeting.

The same applies to organizing transport to any appointment outside the office, or to arranging a day of meetings within the company. Part of your job is to try and give your boss a little breathing space whenever possible, and to organize those little touches which make his life more comfortable. Don't just give up, for instance, if his favourite table in his favourite restaurant is unavailable. Bring your persuasive powers to bear – if he is a good customer they should jolly well give him his favourite table anyway, though you would be too politic to say this in so many words, but you can make sure they get the message.

Your travel agent may be able to help you with tickets for Wimbledon, Ascot, Henley, Cowes, Lord's, Glyndebourne, Covent Garden or the latest popular show, when your boss has left it too late to book through any of the normal channels (he probably doesn't use any of the 'normal' channels, anyway, and may have some 'best friends' of his own in these organizations); and you should certainly be prepared to move heaven and earth to get him what he wants. If you have shown a particular talent for obtaining the tickets or the table, there is a chance that you may occasionally be invited along to his box at Ascot or to dinner at the best restaurant in town – but *don't* count on it!

To add spice to this already spicy pudding, all this organization is also dependent upon no crises arising, and you will find a chapter on these nasty little characters later on (Chapter 11); but if you think and plan ahead as much as possible, you should find that you have given yourself and your boss enough space to do a quick side-step around a crisis and make it to the winning post without too many bruises.

The important thing is tact – to organize your boss without his realizing you are doing it. Don't be bossy – that's his job. Dripping water wears away a stone and in time, gently but firmly, you will train him to do as he's told!

6 *Keeping the Accounts*

We now come to a subject which may very well make some of you wish to skip straight away to the next chapter. Do read this simple section on money matters, however, as you may feel differently when you see how easy bookkeeping can be. It could be that you hate figures and would therefore not consider taking a job where the responsibility for any form of bookkeeping might be yours. On the other hand, if you are reasonably numerate and have a tidy and logical mind, keeping books and working with figures can be very satisfactory and even considerable fun.

As your principal job is that of a secretary and not a bookkeeper, the chances are that you would be required to handle only fairly simple bookkeeping, and we shall therefore discuss here the basic elements of handling the petty cash and writing up the day books. In a small office, you may also be responsible for paying wages, so we have added a small section on this aspect of finance.

Petty Cash

Petty cash is actual money (notes and coin) that is kept in the office, probably in a cash box, to be used for incidental expenses. It is the first thing a thief will look for, so try to find a system that will at least slow down an intruder's ability to get their hands on it.

The amounts needed are usually relatively small, and could well be for any or all of the following:

postage

stationery

taxi, bus or train fares

coffee, tea, etc.

petrol
wages

We have included wages in the above list, as casual or part-time employees could well be paid in cash, especially if they are paid on an hourly basis.

Each receipt of money or expenditure of money should be written down in a petty cash book. If you are starting one, get one big enough to be comfortable to write in. Tiny little notebooks are also easy to misplace. You can use a specially printed petty cash book, a book-keeping book with columns, or just a plain notebook in which you will have to rule analysis columns with the various outgoings listed as headings. An example is set out in Table 1. You will see from the table that the total in the 'amount' column should be equal to all the totals in the other columns. At the end of the month you should reconcile the money you have received (and accounted for) against the money spent. The difference should agree with the amount of cash left in the petty cash box.

Table 1

Cash in hand	Date	Details	Amount	Postage	Stat'y	Fares	Petrol	Wages	Misc.	VAT
£	1985		£	£	£	£	£	£	£	£
200.00	May 1	From bank								
	2	Taxi fare	3.50			3.50				
	3	Postage	34.00	34.00						
	7	Notebooks	3.22		2.80					.42
	10	Envelopes	8.05		7.00					1.05
	13	Bus fare	1.00			1.00				
	15	Coffee	1.50						1.50	
	16	Ms. Smith	32.00					32.00		
	22	Petrol	10.00				8.70			1.30
	24	British Rail	6.00			6.00				
	31	Ms Smith	32.00					32.00		
			131.27	34.00	9.80	10.50	8.70	64.00	1.50	2.77
	31	Balance c/d	68.73							
200.00			200.00							
68.73	Jun. 1	Balance b/d								

Often it doesn't – but don't panic. When this happens, and after you've checked your arithmetic, get advice immediately from another bookkeeper or from someone more experienced at keeping these records. Don't let it go on from month to month hoping that it will magically sort itself out – it won't. Tell your boss. 'I can't get the petty cash to balance' is not a hanging offence.

What has usually happened is that someone has taken some money and forgotten to enter it – or even sometimes the reverse: you forgot to note down the cash that was put in. This is another reason to tell everyone around that you are having difficulty – they may suddenly remember. If you do find out what happened, try to figure out a way of preventing it happening again. If more than one person has access to the petty cash, it can be difficult to sort out errors; if, on the other hand, you are the only person in charge, you must arrange for a substitute whenever you are out of the office.

When you take money from the petty cash box before going shopping (and you will probably take a round sum in pounds to cover the estimated cost), make sure you can return the exact change to the petty cash; similarly, if someone else is taking money from petty cash to purchase something, make sure an IOU is put in at once saying that 'Joan has taken £5'. Then when Joan comes back, exchange the IOU for the receipt from the shop (which should be attached to a petty cash voucher explaining the purchase) plus the change, if any. Receipts should be kept, if possible, for all amounts expended. You can also, of course, pay yourself back from the petty cash if you have already made a purchase on behalf of the office but have paid with your own money.

Sometimes it is allowable for someone to borrow a small sum from petty cash, in which case an IOU should again be kept in the petty cash box until the sum is returned; you should then either return the IOU note to the person or destroy it in front of them. Until you are sure what is acceptable in your office, ask your boss if it is all right to borrow (or lend) the money, but always remember the golden rule: WHENEVER YOU GET OR GIVE MONEY, COUNT IT IMMEDIATELY IN FRONT OF THE OTHER PERSON. This should not cause offence – most people realize it is only done to avoid any misunderstanding later on.

When the petty cash box is getting low, you will need to ask for a cheque to be drawn to cash, so that you can cash it at the bank. You will soon get an idea of how much is usually spent in the course of a month – you want to have enough to prevent you having to keep getting cheques and running to the bank for more cash, but you don't want a larger sum than necessary.

Some people just keep an eye on what's in the box and ask for another cheque when it is running low, but perhaps a better way is the 'imprest' system. You start with an 'imprest' or float of, say, £50, and when at the end of the month you find you have £15 left, you draw a cheque for £35 to bring the float back up to £50 again. In Table 1 above, for instance, a cheque of £131.27 would be cashed to add to the balance of £68.73 to bring the amount of petty cash available to £200 once more.

It is useful to get the money from the bank in notes of small denominations and coins so that you can give the right change when necessary and don't have to have an office whip-round or owe the petty cash 10p because change wasn't available.

As you can see, handling the petty cash accounts is relatively simple, especially if you keep everything up to date. The entries should be made into the petty cash book regularly, probably every two or three days, to make sure the book doesn't get out of date.

Remember, also, to lock up the cash box and put it away immediately after use so as to avoid leaving it on your desk or in another vulnerable place.

Purchase and Sales Journals

Perhaps you are also responsible for all incoming and outgoing invoices in the office. If you are working for a company that actually sells goods, then your duties would probably be heavier than if you handled the day books of a service company, but the principle of entry is essentially the same.

For every purchase the company makes, an entry must be made in a Purchase Journal or Purchase Day Book. The company will obviously have been sent an invoice for the item purchased, and the details of the date, amount, etc., will be taken from this. It is possible that the firm's accountant will want these invoices numbered, so an invoice should be numbered as soon as it arrives, and this number should then be recorded in the Purchase Journal. An example is given below, and you will see that the total amount entered in the 'total' column should amount to the sum of the other columns. You will note that there is a separate column for the VAT content of the article or service purchased.

This example in Table 2 might be typical of a surveyor's office.

Table 2

Date	Details	Invoice No.	Amount	VAT	LEB & Gas	Tel.	Ads	Rent & Rates	Misc.
1985			£	£	£	£	£	£	£
Aug. 8	LEB	1	67.80		67.80				
12	Local Advertiser	2	36.80	4.80			32.00		
20	A. B. Smith Ltd	3	184.00					184.00	
25	British Telecome	4	179.40	23.40		156.00			
26	Post Office	5	34.00						34.00
29	Local Advertiser	6	36.80	4.80			32.00		
			538.80	33.00	67.80	156.00	64.00	184.00	34.00

The Day Book for Sales is very similar; and as you will probably have typed out the invoices yourself as part of your secretarial duties, you can put aside a copy of the invoice to enter into the Sales Day Book. These invoices must also be numbered. An example is set out in Table 3, again for a surveyor.

Table 3

Date	Client	Invoice No.	Total Amount	VAT	Net Amount
1985			£	£	£
Aug. 5	D. Brown	1	149.50	19.50	130.00
9	A. Caldwell	2	230.00	30.00	200.00
15	R. Smith	3	207.00	27.00	180.00
19	A. B. Ltd	4	517.50	67.50	450.00
21	L. Bennett	5	287.50	37.50	250.00
27	T. S. Co. Ltd	6	431.25	56.25	375.00
			1822.75	237.75	1585.00

Table 4

	A. B. Limited 1985				
Dr. Date	Details	Amount	Cr. Date	Details	Amount
		£			£
5/8	Site visit	75.00	4/8	On account	100.00
	VAT	11.25		Balance due	417.50
9/8	Site visit	75.00			
	VAT	11.25			
12/8	Report and Specification	300.00			
	VAT	45.00			
		517.50			517.50

Posting to the Ledger

It is possible that you will be expected to post the information from the Day Books to the Ledger. A Ledger is a record of the state of the individual accounts for each customer or client, and usually at least one page is allotted per client. A typical Ledger page might look like Table 4.

You will see that any expenses paid by the company on behalf of a customer or client will be entered into the client's debit column, and that anything that has been paid *by* the client *to* the company will be entered in the client's credit column. Entries in the Ledger can only be taken from the Day Books, and an appropriate mark or cross-reference must be made on both the Day Book and the Ledger to show that the amount has been posted. This cross-reference is essential in order to avoid the error of posting an amount twice.

The whole point of keeping a Ledger is to record every transaction the company makes with a particular client or customer. This then enables a detailed invoice to be typed up with the information from the Ledger when the time comes to bill the client.

It is probable that the invoices for both sales and purchase transactions will be kept in two separate files, numbered according to the invoice numbers in the Day Books. Once paid, these invoices may then be put into a Paid Invoice file, again a separate file for (a) invoices paid by the company and (b) the company's invoices which have been paid by the clients.

It may be that your bookkeeping duties will not extend to posting to the Ledger, in which case you will hand the Purchase and Sales Day Books to the accountant or bookkeeper on a regular basis.

Wages

One of your secretarial duties might well be to pay the wages. This would probably mean using the PAYE (Pay As You Earn) system. The process of paying wages under the PAYE system means deducting tax at source, and you would therefore need a supply of tax tables from the Inland Revenue.

The wages might be paid weekly or monthly, and an hour or two should be set aside for this purpose. Every time an employee is paid, he or she receives a pay slip which shows in detail how the actual amount paid to them is arrived at. Essentially, the net wage is the gross wage less deductions.

Added to the basic wage might be an amount for overtime work. From this gross figure would be deducted amounts for (a) income tax (PAYE) and (b) national insurance. National insurance provides benefits principally for unemployment, sickness and old-age pensions. The employer is responsible for paying the greater proportion of national insurance, with the employee contributing a smaller proportion each week, the amount to be paid depending on the basic salary. Contribution tables, supplied by the DHSS, state clearly the amount to be paid each week by employer and employee.

As stated earlier, there are tax tables for calculating the PAYE deductions. These tables are normally supplied to the company by the local tax office. If you are responsible for paying wages and salaries to several employees in the company, it might be a good idea to visit the office of the local Inspector of Taxes for advice on how to use the tax tables. Alternatively, your company's accountant could well show you how to do this and refer you to the appropriate tables for the various employees. Each employee is allotted a tax code by the Inland Revenue, and this code determines the amount of tax to be paid. It would also be worthwhile acquiring a copy of 'The Employer's Guide to National Insurance Contributions' and 'The Employer's Guide to PAYE'.

Paying Bills

Perhaps your responsibility ends with sending a bill on to the accounts department. If so, they will tell you what procedures they want you to follow. However if *you* are responsible for payment, you will probably put it into an Unpaid Bills file. In either case, you will want to make sure that the bill or invoice is correct. Were the goods or services actually received? If you have an ordering system, does the bill agree with what was ordered? When you receive an invoice, check to make sure that it is right. Find out if the goods really have been both ordered and received.

If you do not have a formal purchase order system whereby a form has to be filled in and the purchase authorized before ordering, you should keep a record of what goods are ordered – particularly if they have been ordered by phone and consequently no paperwork exists. Write it all down and keep it (perhaps in the Unpaid Bills file) until you can attach your own record to a delivery note and eventually to the invoice.

When goods are dispatched, they usually come with a delivery note which lists the contents of the order and leaves a space for you to sign, saying that you have in fact received them. These delivery notes should be kept so that they can be compared with the invoice that will arrive later.

If you do not pay business bills in the month they are received, you will get a statement at the end of the month giving a brief listing of all invoices that have not been paid. In these computerized days, it may well show all purchases, all payments, and all amounts outstanding. When you get a statement, staple it to the invoice or invoices it refers to. The statement is only a summary which has to be explained by the invoice itself.

If you get a statement for which you cannot find the invoice, or a letter demanding payment which you cannot relate to an unpaid bill, ring up the supplier and ask for a copy of the original invoice. Apologize and tell them you can't understand how it has happened, but you cannot find the original invoice and need a copy to sort the matter out. Don't be bullied by demands for payment into issuing a cheque in payment of a bill that you are not sure you owe.

You must, of course, look through your Paid Bills file or your chequebook to make sure that the bill really has not been paid. Mistakes happen, and even the post goes astray sometimes. If you think the bill has been paid, you will be able to write a letter saying so. Give the number and date of the cheque. If they write back and say that the cheque was not received, you will have to ask your bank if the cheque was paid and, if not, to stop payment on it so that no one can use it. Banks make a charge for stopping payment, so be sure that this is necessary before instructing your bank in this way.

When a bill comes in, look to see if there is an offer of a discount if the bill is paid within a certain time. This discount reduces the bill by a small percentage in exchange for immediate payment. Ask your boss if he wishes to take advantage of this offer; if he does, make sure that the bill is paid immediately, or at least within the time limit.

Generally speaking, you have to find out what practice your boss wants to follow with regard to paying bills. Some people pay them immediately, some people pay everything in the Unpaid Bills file at the end of the month, or on a certain regular date, or when they have received a substantial amount of income, and some people don't pay anything until they receive overdue notices or threats.

If you make out cheques, be sure they are properly filled in. Make sure the date is right – in January be very careful you are not still using last year's date. (It's a good idea to fill in the correct year on a few cheques in advance in January, until you get used to the number of the new year.) Make sure you start writing the amount at the extreme left of the cheque so that nothing can be added before it. If you make a mistake, it can be corrected if the correction is initialled (or, in some cases, signed – read the inside of your chequebook or ask the bank for advice) by the person signing it. But if it looks too confusing, write 'cancelled' on the cheque and the stub, and start again.

Fill in the cheque stub or the appropriate line in the chequebook with all the information you have written on the cheque, and if there is room it is useful to note what the payment is for.

When you post the cheque, send back with it sufficient information about the bill you are paying. Some people send you invoices in duplicate and ask for one copy back. Some have a part of the bill that should be torn off and returned. If there is nothing like that with the invoice, use a comp slip or a small note to tell them their invoice number, if there is one, or giving sufficient information so that they know what bill you are paying.

Other means of payment

In addition to sending a cheque, there are other means of making payments.

You can authorize your bank, by a form known as a Standing Order, to pay a certain sum to a certain person or firm at regular intervals. You might want (or be required by your lease) to pay the rent this way each month. No notification will be sent to you, but your bank statement each month will show the payment (in the same column as the cheques paid) with a code SO to indicate that the amount was paid by Standing Order.

There is also a means of authorizing your bank to pay a varying sum to someone at regular intervals. This is known as a Direct Debit, and can be used for regular bills that may vary in amount, such as bills for various utilities. In this case, you normally receive a bill showing the amount that will be debited (withdrawn) from your account, but you do not have to issue a cheque to pay it. It will be shown on your bank statement with coding 'DD'.

Make sure that you know which standing orders or direct debits have been authorized, and check up on them each month to see that the correct payment has been made.

If you have to send money abroad, you may have to make payment in a currency other than pounds sterling. Your bank can supply you with a cheque in whatever currency you need, and will make a small charge for this service. You can look in the newspaper (financial pages) to find out the exchange rate in advance, or ring any bank. These rates fluctuate constantly, so you won't know until your bank issues a cheque in a foreign currency exactly how much it will cost in pounds.

Your bank will also be able to provide foreign money if your boss is going abroad – but let them know in advance if you can, as local branches don't always keep a large supply of every currency. Remember to get an assortment of notes and coins, so that he will not have to try to change a large note for his first purchase, which may be a small one. They will also issue traveller's cheques, which you pay for in pounds and which can be exchanged for local currency all over the world.

Don't forget that the Post Office also offers many banking facilities, including being able to pay bills without cheques by Giro and making payments overseas. It is also a good idea to buy a postal order to pay small amounts instead of issuing a cheque for, say, 30p (the Post Office makes a small charge in addition to the value of the postal order). And if you want to provide someone overseas with the postage to reply to you, you can buy an international voucher for this purpose. Read their brochures or ring the Post Office and ask about their services.

Many businesses will let you pay for a purchase with a credit card, even if you are ordering by phone. You must be able to quote the number and expiry date of the card, and they will usually insist that the goods be sent to the address of the cardholder.

In every case in which you hand over cash or make payment of any kind – get a receipt. The only time when this is not customary is when paying bills by mail with a cheque (though even here you can ask to have a receipt sent back to you).

Computerized Accounts

Many companies, including quite small businesses, keep their accounts on a computer. We are not going to discuss computerized systems in this chapter, but computing is just another area which might become part of a secretary's duties alongside word processing.

As you can see, the bookkeeping duties described above should not prove too onerous and could well be fitted into a day's or week's schedule if they are part of your responsibilities as a secretary. Bookkeeping is more likely to be part of a secretary's job in a one-girl office or small company. Very often in small businesses, an accountant is employed on a freelance basis and may well take the books away only once a month to bring them up to date. This responsibility could, therefore, give you invaluable experience and might well prove to be a great asset for the future, should you ever consider starting a small company or running a business of your own.

Naturally, great accuracy is called for when dealing with figures. A calculator is essential – but so is common sense. A quick appraisal of the figures should reveal whether or not they appear to be accurate.

We do hope that this chapter will encourage you to consider taking employment where a knowledge of figure work is required; certainly your range of job suitability will be considerably widened if you can accept this added responsibility.

There are many teach-yourself books on the subject of simple accounting and bookkeeping, including one in the Penguin Self-Starter series – although there is nothing quite as instructive as practical experience. Hence the desirability of handling the accounts in a small office if you have the opportunity, and you would be strongly advised not to dismiss bookkeeping through a fear of figures, but to 'give it a go'.

Your initial training as a secretary should have covered the basics of bookkeeping. Generally, even the smallest office will have a bookkeeper who comes in at least once a week to keep the books in order. However, the most delightfully scatty bosses, who make most of their notes on the backs of envelopes, can cause real headaches for their accountants by not keeping their books in order; and if you, as the secretary/bookkeeper (where there is no bookkeeper as such), can take over that function, you will keep the accountant happy as well as your boss, and the latter will have to pay considerably less in accountancy fees than he did when chaos reigned. With you there, even without a bookkeeper, the books should be kept under control.

Listen carefully when the accountant tells you what he wants, and make notes at the same time, so that even without formal bookkeeping training you will be able to handle the books in a businesslike manner.

7 *People Are My Best Friends*

You will realize from Chapter 5, Organizing Your Boss, that, at least from the travel point of view, much of your efficiency relies heavily on a good relationship with a pet travel agent. For the rest, though, it would appear to be entirely up to you and your systems. Well, systems are indeed lovesome things, as we have said, and you should love and respect yours; but the efficiency or otherwise of a senior secretary depends very largely on her relationship with people who, while they may appear to be further down the work scale than she is, actually provide the vital buttresses without which her efficient edifice would crumble hopelessly.

As a secretary, your most important Best Friends are:

(a) The telephone operator/switchboard girl
(b) The post boy
(c) The lady in Petty Cash/Accounts, and
(d) The kitchen staff.

We are not forgetting the travel agent, who can be your best friend in another capacity also, but we will talk about that later.

The reasons for the above people being so important to you should be self-evident. You will have an ally (a) when, at a quarter past six on a Friday, your boss decides he *must* speak urgently to someone in Bolivia to which there is no dialling code, so you have to wrestle with international exchanges. You will have someone (b) willing to hold up the mail or make a special collection from you as you wildly type the last page of the urgent eight-page letter that must go off tonight and wasn't dictated to you until five o'clock. You will be able to get your boss £50 (c) to tide him over until the banks open, or the machine regurgitates his Cashcard which it snicked out of his fingers and refused to return. Last but not least, you will be able to get him and/or that important visitor coffee, tea, sandwiches or a plate of ham and salad at any given moment, whether or not the firm's canteen (d) is officially shut.

The people who run these invaluable services must be won over, befriended, not patronized. Do not fall into the trap of thinking that because you are the managing director's secretary you are more important than they are – you are not – they are infinitely more important than you. They are your lifeline, and without them you are almost helpless. With them on your side, you are half-way towards creating the impression of being an efficient secretary who is capable of applying the right salve to the current crisis.

'Friendship' is the key word. That is the only way the relationship can truly work, whether you are in charge of a team of junior secretaries, or one girl trying to run one man's life. They have got to like you, and you must like them and give them your time. By all means be too busy to gossip to the finance director, but never be too busy to listen to the post boy's woes. If time is really of the essence, escape into the Ladies' loo when you see him looming on the horizon, but don't give him the brushoff face to face.

This is not to say, of course, that you should sit around for hours gossiping – in fact, *you* shouldn't gossip at all. Confidentiality is your karma, and if people try to pump you, act dumb in both senses of the word. But be a good listener, and be humble. If you are the senior secretary, don't behave as if you know you are; no one is going to chat to someone who is 'above it all', and, apart from the sheer mechanics of people's usefulness to you, it is another aspect of your job to pick up judicious snippets of office tattle. The more senior a man or woman becomes, the more isolated they are. You must be able to keep your boss abreast of what is happening to people in the company – marriages, births, deaths, worries, likes or dislikes and, most importantly, opinions in general of company policies or changes.

A fine balance must be struck, however, between your confidential status as senior secretary and mucking in with the crowd. As you become more senior, so your responsibilities increase, your work load is more varied and almost certainly more confidential, and you may even be entrusted with taking certain decisions on your own. Somehow you must manage to tread the thin line without falling over into one camp or the other; but there is no easy advice on how to do this. It really is a question of acquiring a 'feel', an instinctive wisdom for how far to be one of the girls, while at the same time retaining a certain privacy for yourself and your boss.

Something else for which there is no easy advice is the matter of personal hygiene; as a senior secretary, you may be faced with having to talk to someone about this delicate subject. It can't be left to your boss, and if you don't deal with it he may well have to ask you to do so. It may result in the person in question not speaking to you for a while, but it is all a question of diplomacy and tact. The good secretary should have both.

Try: 'Have you noticed how deodorants don't seem to work so well on sticky days/in hot rooms? I often wonder about mine. They go off sometimes, you know, and it's worse when you're feeling nervous, isn't it? I hate to have to mention it, but it can be hard for someone new in this office, and I thought I should tell you . . .'

Or: 'Perhaps it's the time of the month – you can often tell when someone's "on" can't you? . . .'

There is no polite way of telling someone that they smell, but, whatever you say and however you solve it, it has to be handled, so – brace yourself and do it! By the way, don't get complacent about yourself in that direction. It is always possible that you are the offender – even if only occasionally . . . once a month, perhaps?

One further word about your travel agent. Most deal with theatre tickets as well as with travel arrangements, and often keep blocks of tickets in hand, especially for very popular shows.

So you find yourself landed with the chairman of the Japanese connection, with whom your boss is about to effect the most enormous and lucrative deal, and the visitor has inscrutably and unexpectedly turned up with his wife and two daughters in tow. Your boss, desperate to entertain him in the finest manner, has roped in *his* wife, and his son and one of the company's eligible bachelor executives as escorts for the daughters – but it turns out that there is only one thing the Japanese connection really wants to do and that is to see the new Lloyd Webber musical . . . tonight . . . *eight* tickets!

Cry on the shoulder of your travel agent, and the chances are he will come up trumps. Your boss is proud of you, but you know it isn't really *you*, it's your wonderful, friendly travel agent.

So befriend him, nurture him, take him out to lunch, spoil him, send him a bottle of good sherry at Christmas, or (if 'he' is a woman) a dozen red roses in your boss's name – to hell with the expense, your travel agent is a priceless commodity. If your boss questions the cost, remind him about the tickets for the Lloyd Webber show.

Of course, you may work for one man running a tiny business with no huge deals in Japan, no company kitchen, no post boy, none of the situations mentioned above, in which case you may say that none of this has anything to do with you – but it has. You still come across people who operate services vital to your efficient operation. You must still take your letters to the local post office, pay in petty cash at the local bank, buy newspapers from the vendor on the corner, get your stationery and office equipment from local suppliers, buy provisions for business lunches from the local delicatessen – all of which will be done more quickly, pleasantly (and, in some cases, cheaply!) if they are your friends.

And as for the telephone: if you have ever spent twenty minutes shouting futilely at an exchange operator who, having stoically listened to your invective, then pulls out the lead, leaving you to rant to inky black silence – you will know the value of making the right friends!

8 *That's Entertainment!*

Don't panic – it's very unlikely that you would be expected to cook and serve a five-course Cordon Bleu lunch for twelve; but there are many aspects of entertainment that you may come across, from coffee and biscuits for two to drinks and buffet lunch for a board meeting.

Serving drinks, in particular, is something that, even in this non-discriminating age, women seldom have to do unless they are trained barmaids – or senior secretaries! It is quite tricky to get the proportions right when you first start having to measure out mixed drinks, especially as most office glasses are a plain, workaday type without any kind of pattern to measure against. You may either get complaints that the drinks are too weak, or you will have them all stretched out on the floor, pole-axed by your Mickey Finns – until you get your 'eye' in, it's as well to ask each person to guide you as you are pouring. If someone asks you for some concoction you have never heard of and have no idea how to make, ask them – you're not a barmaid, after all . . . Be warned: some people (especially men) are *extremely* fussy about dry martinis. If you come across one of these, let him instruct you.

The situation we are considering at the moment is most likely to be drinks after a Board meeting or something similar, and this will probably take place in an ante-room near the boardroom, in which there is a drinks cupboard. It is best to get out all the bottles and glasses you will need (and a few more just in case), rather than scrabbling about inside the cupboard. If there is a large table in the ante-room, use that as your 'bar', covering it with a paper cloth first to protect it against spills. Set out the spirits on one side, the mixers beside them, then the squashes and soft drinks, and then the sherries and aperitifs. It looks nice if this arrangement is in a kind of crescent shape, and everything is easier to reach. Arrange the glasses in front in a similar way, with the tumblers for the spirits on one side and the sherry glasses on the other. An advantage of the crescent arrangement is that you have an empty space in the middle to work in.

Your firm's boardroom may have a proper bar, of course, in which case your troubles are fewer. The trickiest situation is if you have to wheel everything into the boardroom on a trolley: tricky, partly because it's never easy to know quite when they have finished their meeting, partly because even the best-designed trolleys seem to have a will of their own, and most of all because of space. The best way to get over the last problem is to put the glasses on the bottom shelf and the bottles on the top, leaving yourself as much space as possible to work on. (Yes, the glasses *should* be on the bottom shelf – it is much easier to bring one glass at a time to the top and fill it with the contents of the bottles to hand than to do things the other way around.) Here it is even more important to arrange both the bottles and the glasses in a logical order so that you know exactly where everything is and can reach it easily. In all events, cover the trolley with a paper cloth, and have some kichen roll with you to mop up any spills.

Talking of spills, if the worst happens and you tip Martini Rosso all over the pale-honey-coloured carpet, a good squirt from the soda syphon, *then* mop it up, then another squirt of soda, should undo most of the damage. It is important to squirt the soda first so as to dilute the colour of the spillage as much as possible.

In most larger companies any catering will be done by the canteen staff, including preparing sandwiches for a visitor or a light lunch for someone in his office, and if you have made Best Friends with the kitchen staff beforehand – as you should – the visitor/boss will have lots of smoked salmon in the sandwiches or a larger wedge of game pie, it will arrive earlier rather than later and will be prettily decorated with parsley.

If, however, you work for a very small team, you may on occasion be asked to put together a buffet lunch for a meeting with an important client. This does not mean you will have to spend the morning cooking! Rather, it will entail an enjoyable hour at the local delicatessen allowing yourself to go slightly mad with the office expenses (only slightly – don't buy a sixteen-ounce jar of caviar). Nevertheless, you are not laying on a banquet – four or five good cheeses, a variety of cold meats or pâté, some fresh fruit and a mixed salad will be more than adequate; don't forget, also, some fresh French bread and various salad dressings, mustards and pickles. These store very well, anyway, and can be kept for the next time.

There will probably already be some sort of crockery in the office, but if you have to invest in some, keep it simple – plain white is probably best, since matching replacements are easier to obtain – riots of little roses are not really suitable for an office environment. Remember to get some small ramekins or dishes suitable for decanting the mustards and pickles into – don't just dump the jars on the table!

While you have the office purse in your hand, invest in some disposable tablecloths with matching napkins. Again a plain colour is usually best for office use, either a colour which tones with the office décor, or plain white. Then, with everything nicely laid and perhaps a small vase of flowers, or a flowering plant, in the centre, you will have presented a very attractive table for a working lunch.

In this situation it is unlikely that you will have to deal with drinks. Most men nowadays prefer to drink in moderation at lunchtime, or even not to drink at all. Depending on the number of people present, buy one or two bottles of a light, white wine, and a large bottle or two of mineral water.

As a senior secretary, there is another aspect of entertaining for your boss which may confront you – taking someone out to dinner at a restaurant. This does not happen very often, being really the preserve of the Personal Assistant, about whom we shall talk a little in Chapter 13 on Promotion or Staying Put, p. 102, but nevertheless it is worth discussing because some senior secretaries do have to take people out on their employer's behalf.

Let's imagine you have to entertain the managing director of one of your firm's overseas subsidiaries, take him to the theatre and out to dinner afterwards – on your own because your boss is away. Many men still find it embarrassing to be taken out by a woman, especially a non-executive one, so you must make sure all the wheels run very smoothly. Any small hitch, and he will start taking over as a natural male reaction – this is disastrous when you consider that, as *you* are taking *him* out, *you* are paying, and if you have allowed the role reversal to slip you will find at the end of the evening that he has whipped out his American Express card and paid the restaurant bill before you have time to blink – and that is not the object of the exercise.

So be very organized. Plan out your routes beforehand: whether you will travel to the theatre by taxi or by car, and, if the latter, where you will park; what time you should collect your guest from his hotel in order to make the theatre in plenty of time. Always add at least ten minutes extra to the time you *think* it will take, to allow for traffic jams, parking problems, or other horrors: he might even turn up with an unexpected girlfriend (see Chapter 11 on Crises)! Check how far the restaurant is from the theatre, that is, whether you will be able to walk a short way (preferable), or whether you will have to recover the car or get another taxi. Also make sure, if you are going by car and plan to park it in an underground garage, that you know what time that garage closes – try not to choose one that shuts at eleven o'clock at night, or you will be faced with no transport home! If you have decided to travel by taxi, make sure that you will be able to find one late in the evening to take you back to your guest's hotel or, better still, arrange beforehand for a mini-cab to collect you at, say, midnight from the restaurant. (This may not leave you much time for the meal if the restaurant you have chosen is some way from the theatre; you may not start your meal until after eleven, and you do not want to rush it. You should allow yourselves at least an hour and a half at the restaurant, preferably even a bit longer, so work this out in advance too, in order to have the mini-cab waiting at the right time.)

The theatre tickets will presumably be no problem, since you will have organized them previously with your Best Friend Travel Agent; when you get to the theatre, however, have a word with the barman before the show starts and order drinks for the interval. Most theatres allow for this, and it saves a horrible crush. It is quite possible that your overseas director will insist on buying you a drink before the show – let him, as a sop to his male vanity, but if he is the company's (i.e. your) guest, this is the *only* thing he should pay for.

Dealing with the bill in the restaurant can be the most difficult business if you don't get a grip on the situation from the beginning. Preferably you should have booked the table in *your* name on behalf of your company, and at the same time mentioned that you would be expecting to pay the bill at the end of the meal. On arrival, however, hang back a little while leaving your coat or make some excuse for a momentary absence, beard the head waiter and remind him that *you* are paying tonight, on behalf of your firm; then, at the end of the meal, catch the waiter's eye to ensure he hands the bill to you.

As so often happens in this age of sexual 'equality', a woman has to work twice as hard as a man would have to in order to take charge of the situation. After all, if a man makes a hash of taking a woman out, it may be irritating but she is hardly likely to take over the reins. Nevertheless, don't be panicked by the thought of it all – like most things, it's really very simple if you are well organized beforehand, and there is no reason why you should not be able to entertain very adequately on your boss's behalf.

In fact, he may be mystified to discover that his overseas colleagues prefer to visit when he's away!

9 *Meetings and Minutes*

The arranging and attending of meetings, and the taking of Minutes, can be one of the most daunting tasks to confront you, especially when you are new and don't know half the faces round the table. It *must* all be done properly, especially the Minutes, as these are the records for years to come of all company policy decisions great and small.

First, though, the meeting must be arranged. The date of a large meeting (let's, for the sake of argument, call it a board meeting) will probably be arranged at the end of the previous meeting when everybody concerned is present with their diaries available – or sometimes they are prearranged at the beginning of the year at, say, monthly intervals. There may, however, be an extraordinary meeting called to deal with some special item, and if it is your boss who calls the meeting, you will have to find a date suitable to all the parties. To get more than two busy men to agree to meet on a day that suits all of them is little short of a miracle, and since board meetings usually involve about twelve busy men, you can see that this situation is one of the senior secretary's best-known nightmares.

Get at least three possible dates from your boss first, then ratify these with the most senior directors, or people whose presence is absolutely vital. If, wonder of wonders, you actually manage to settle on one date that is suitable to all these people, then you can concentrate on the lesser mortals who should be there but whose presence is not quite so essential. Don't necessarily be sidetracked by someone's title: depending on the subject of the meeting, it may be far more important to have the machinists' shop steward there than the company chairman, who can be kept informed of the proceedings by a senior colleague.

Once the meeting has been arranged, you should send out confirmation of it, stating clearly the date, time and place it will be held, and enclosing the agenda at the same time. If the meeting is a few weeks hence, send out a reminder note nearer the time, and check with all the probable participants, or their secretaries, that they plan to attend; if any of them do not, remember that their names go in the 'Apologies for Absence' section of the Minutes, and that they will still require copies of the Minutes when they are circulated. You should already have a special shorthand notebook for Minutes, and as the time of the meeting draws near, keep this accessible to jot down any apologies for absence or other notes you might have to bring up with your boss before the meeting starts.

The layout of a board meeting table varies from company to company, and some managements are very casual and laid back about it; but there is a formal way which it is useful to know about. Each person has a clean blotter on which there is a selection of sharpened pencils and pens – biros (that work!), felt-tips (ditto) or markers if necessary – a fresh lined pad about A4 size for taking notes, a copy of the agenda if they have not received this beforehand, and copies of any other relevant papers they may need during the meeting.

The chairman of the meeting (not necessarily the chairman of the company) sits at the head of the table with the committee officers on either side of him, i.e. the vice chairman or managing director, the treasurer and the secretary – that's not necessarily you. If it is a board meeting, the Secretary (with a capital S) will be the Company Secretary, who will not take the Minutes. You will, and you should sit close to the chairman so that you can ask him questions, or he can direct you, at any point, without disrupting proceedings by having to shout down miles of polished mahogany. You may not even sit at the table at all, but in a chair slightly behind the chairman, between him and the vice chairman or the next most senior officer.

Don't arrive late, no matter how busy you are. Nothing takes precedence in an office over a large meeting, and if you are taking the Minutes, the meeting cannot start without you. You should, in any case, have arrived a few minutes before anybody else to check last-minute details – has everybody been included and does each person have everything he needs; is mid-way coffee organized and readily available; are there ashtrays available; if there is to be some kind of presentation requiring slides is the screen at hand and in the right place, and the projector, and the slides; should there be a sound system and, if so, is it properly set up; if the proceedings are to be taped as well as recorded by your Minute-taking is the recorder present and in working order; has the technician arrived, and has he got somewhere suitable to sit; do all the lights work; is the telephone connected, or disconnected, as preferred; has the kitchen been primed to bring up sandwiches at 12.30; last, but by no means least, is the room *clean*?

Just before you go through this list, don't neglect yourself. Have you got everything: your shorthand pad with plenty of fresh pages; a good supply of sharp pencils in case one breaks, or shorthand pens if you use them; a copy of the agenda; the Minute Book; the list of those who cannot be present, together with any points they wished to mention.

One other thing which may seem odd to talk about but can cause you untold misery: remember to go to the loo before you get trapped in there. Other members of the committee can make some excuse to leave for a few moments, but you really cannot, and nothing is worse than trying to concentrate on what people are saying while in the grip of a desperate need which cannot possibly be relieved for at least two hours. Also, if you have a cold or a cough, you can guarantee that your nose will begin to stream, or an uncontrollable tickle will get you in the back of the throat, at a crucial moment in the meeting. Take ample supplies of tissues and cough lozenges, and make sure you can get at them easily. If they are there, you may not need them; if they are not, you surely will!

The actual taking of Minutes is not as frightening as it sounds. You do not have to take everything down verbatim, and as you get more used to it (and to the people on the committee) you will learn by experience what you can leave out. Minutes are not necessarily best taken in shorthand; if you try and get down every word in shorthand, you may be dedicating all your brainpower to getting the outlines right, whereas you will produce a better result if you summarize the proceedings at the time, especially as you will probably understand it better if you listen, instead of trying to write the whole time. If your shorthand is rusty (or even if it is not), Minutes are best recorded using a fair amount of longhand, so take heart. In fact, there are often names to get right which must be spelt carefully in longhand. This is where it is important for you to be sitting near the chairman, so that you can ask him for any name spellings you are not sure of, or even ask: 'Do you want me to Minute that?' if some remark seems to be rather irrelevant.

At the end of each subject on the agenda, the chairman will wind up the discussion with a brief summing-up of the proceedings (rather like a judge's at the end of a trial), and maybe a request for some action to a committee member. You should take down as much of this as you can, as this is the 'gist' for which you have been waiting, and you *must* record the request for action and who it is directed to. The chairman's comments will help you to cut through mountains of twaddle and waffle, but don't précis too much. People like their comments to be recorded in black and white, so you should be careful to give them their credits, even in a slightly truncated version.

The layout for Minutes is usually based on the example shown, with variations. Under the heading of Action, the initials of the participant expected to take action on the matter under discussion should be typed. Sometimes it may be felt prudent to indicate to such a participant that his name has been marked for such action in the Minutes, perhaps in a covering letter. A gentle reminder sometimes prompts a response which might otherwise be slow in appearing.

Don't delay with transcribing your shorthand, first of all because obviously you will need to rely to a certain extent on your memory, but more importantly because the committee will need to have the decisions and issues in front of them in black and white as quickly as possible, particularly if they are to take any action before the next meeting. Minutes should be circulated not later than about five days after a meeting, unless there is an exemplary reason why they cannot be, and this includes the time taken to do the first draft, clear it with the chairman, and type and photocopy the definitive version – bearing in mind that in the interim the chairman will have gone off for a long weekend's grouse-shooting! In some companies, the Minutes are also circulated to all committee members for approval *before* the definitive version is put into the Minute Book, so you may have to allow for this time lag as well.

Once the Minutes have been circulated, your job, as far as they are concerned, is over – until the next time – but you should keep a

MINUTES OF THE MEETING OF THE PLANNING GROUP HELD ON
29th February 1903
at the Burglars' Hall, London S3

Present ACTION

Mr T. P. Fotheringay (Chairman)
Mr R. H. Fotheringay (Vice-Chairman)
Mr S. D. Mornington (Sales)
Mr D. I. Y. Swindle (Accounts)
Miss D. Mure (Secretary)

Apologies for Absence

Apologies for absence received from:
Mr D. Pearce, Mr W. P. Fraser

Minutes of Last Meeting

The Minutes of the last meeting were read and approved.

Matters Arising

There were no matters arising from the Minutes
of the last meeting.

Chairman's Report

The Chairman presented his report to the meeting and
made the following points:
(insert points and action if applicable.)

Accounts

Mr Swindle passed round copies of the accounts
for members to peruse.

Election of Officers*

The following nominations had been received:
Mr T. P. Fotheringay - Chairman,
Mr R. H. Fotheringay - Vice-Chairman

There being no other nominations and the candidates
being eligible, the above were duly elected.

Consideration of the New Computerized Accounts Scheme

A lengthy discussion took place and it was decided to refer the matter to Mr Swindle's department for further consideration DIYS

(Other items on the Agenda and action)

Any Other Business

Date of Next Meeting

The next meeting will take place on the
31st September 1903 in the Burglars' Hall at 2.30pm

***This only at Annual General Meetings.**

good, clean, fair copy yourself, even if your boss has a copy of his own. In the intervening weeks he may jot little pencil notes all over his copy; you may need to make another photocopy for someone who has lost his; anyway, it is always better to have one or two spares just in case, and yours may end up being the only unsullied copy to be put in the Minute Book.

By rights, the version which is finally signed and entered in the Minute Book should be the original fair copy; but if this has been kept by the chairman, who has scribbled all over it (one chairman we know used to nibble the corners off his!), then of course a photo copy will have to do.

The Minute Books (there will be more than one unless the company is less than a year old) are the company records of every board meeting (or meeting of a main body) from the very start, and must be kept safely. They are usually kept by the Company Secretary (in a large company he will monitor their safekeeping in the archives), and should *never* be thrown out. Other members of the committee will probably keep their copies for some time, too, but they are not obliged to hang on to them indefinitely. If it is your duty to look after the current Minute Book, you must keep it in your office in a lockable cupboard and always have it to hand for each meeting. At the beginning of each meeting, the Minutes of the previous meeting will be formally approved and signed by the committee chairman, treasurer and secretary, after which they should immediately be placed into the Minute Book in date order, in front of the committee so that they can all see it has been done.

Before the next meeting (even if the meetings are prearranged on a monthly basis) you should send out a reminder to all concerned, as you would do for an extraordinary meeting. This can be in the form of the agenda for the next meeting or, if the agenda is not finalized until the last minute, just a short note. Make sure the recipients get the reminder at least five days before the date of the meeting so they have time, if they wish, to ask for something to be put on the agenda, to make their apologies, or just to get themselves organized beforehand.

Recordings

Large conferences are a different kettle of fish (more in Chapter 17, under Major Conferences, p. 125), but even at quite small meetings at which you may be taking Minutes, your boss may require a recording, particularly if the meeting is of special importance, and you may have to arrange for recording equipment (and a technician, perhaps) to attend. There are specialists in this field, and this is a task that should not be handled by a friend who is good with the tape recorder.

Continuity Note

Whatever the size of the meeting, if a tape recording is being made, a continuity note must be kept, with the title of the meeting on it, indicating beyond all possible error:

(i) number of tape
(ii) side A or B (or 1 or 2)
(iii) date and time of start of *each* side
(iv) name of *each* speaker and
(v) time of each speaker's contribution (including interjections from the floor)

For later transcription, it is better for the recording to be on audio cassette (ordinary music-style), but make sure that only cassettes up to ninety minutes (C. 90s) are used. With anything longer, the tape is too thin and may break when it is being transcribed (foot-pedal and earphone transcription machines cause a strong pull on the tape and it may snap under the pressure).

For transcribing, cassette/audio machines with foot-pedals and earphones are much more common than reel-to-reel machines with such facilities, and you could encounter problems if your boss insists on using only a reel-to-reel machine (ideally, there should be both, the reel-to-reel tapes being used as back-up).

Transcripts

When you are asked to transcribe recorded tapes from a meeting, they should be typed in double spacing, with speakers' names or initials in the left margin in capitals, and every word should be taken from the tape and put on to paper, unless you are editing at the same time, in which case you make decisions as you go along about what to include. The top of the first page of typing could look like this:

Transcript of meeting of
International Burglars' Association, 12–15 May 1999
Day One, Session One. 10 am till 12 noon.

Tape 1, Side A /bb

Follow-on pages should look like this:

Tape 1, Side B 2/bb

CH: Although I am unable to discern any appreciable improvement in the sales of steel tubes over the past year (unintelligible) I should like . . .
BS: May I interject, for a moment?
Chair: I should prefer this to wait until the speaker has finished his remarks.

and

Tape 2, Side A 17/bb

The page number followed by your initials is best, with pagination right through at least for each tape. It is very important to be able to sort out which transcript belongs to which tape at the end. Make sure, when transcribing from the tapes, that you use a copy of the continuity note and keep referring to it, in combination with the programme, advance copies of papers which were presented to the meeting (especially for technical words and phrases, etc.) and the list of participants (for getting the names right!).

If foreign languages (see also Chapter 17, under Interpreters, p. 130) are on the tape, you may wish to have someone transcribe in the foreign language and then get it translated; alternatively, it may be possible for someone to type and translate it in one go, editing as they go along. Recordings should, if possible, be made all in English, which means ensuring that the *interpreted* English from, say, French, is recorded, not the original French, but the *original* English is recorded, *not* the interpreted French. If this is done, it may be necessary to obtain the interpreter's consent to his/her words being recorded since they are, in fact, copyright.

For a large-scale conference, the recording firm should know how to handle this and should ensure that their cabling and wiring is carried out correctly in accordance with *your* instructions; make sure you make your requirements clear, as they will not necessarily do it the way you want them to without explicit direction. Further information on this, too, can be found in Chapter 17, under Interpreters.

10 *Letters and Correspondence*

We live in a hurried age. Gone are the days when people wrote vivid accounts of their daily lives, couched in elegant terms just begging to be read at leisure. Even so, a letter, albeit a business letter, should invite the recipient to sit back in his chair and give it some attention. Your employer's closest friend will be unimpressed upon receiving a letter full of spelling and grammatical mistakes.

Spelling

Good spelling is something which comes naturally to some people, not at all to others. If you are in the second category, arm yourself with a good dictionary which is keeping up with the times (a dictionary doesn't have to be many years old to lack terms from today's technology, for example), and be ruthless with yourself. Even if you are a good speller, check your spelling occasionally; you can sometimes suddenly get a blind spot about a word used regularly, or find that you have always spelled something wrongly without realizing. Don't be lazy about this – bad spelling may be regarded as charming in gossipy letters to a friend, but in business correspondence it is far less forgivable. Your boss is allowed to be a bad speller – your brief is to correct it. Your boss is also allowed to be rotten at basic English grammar but, again, you are not. We discuss a few fundamental grammatical rules in this chapter; if you feel your grammar is shaky, buy a book and brush up on it.

Grammar

You may think this is over-stressing the case; but your ability to edit your employer's correspondence into something which is readable, if not actually elegant, is important to the image of the boss himself, the company, and you; and just as a smart reception area or a polite telephonist projects a good image, so your letters, neatly typed and couched in good English, reflect the high standards the company insists upon.

English grammar is very easy when compared with the grammar of other languages. We have a neutral definite and indefinite article ('the' and 'a' are always the same, whether we are talking about tables and chairs or men and women); our verbs and adverbs are logically placed, as are our adjectives, not stuck on to the end of a long sentence or squeezed between a pronoun and a verb; and our verb tenses are relatively straightforward . . . so you would not think it too much to expect native British speakers to get right the few grammatical rules we do have. Unfortunately, the use of good grammar grows sloppier all the time, so that when a letter arrives that is well phrased and punctuated, it comes as a pleasant surprise.

The comma

For example, check your use of commas by reading aloud the letter you have just typed (if you can do so without the rest of the office thinking you've gone mad). If your sentences leave you black in the face long before their end, you should have put a comma in somewhere; if, on the other hand, you sound as if you have a bad case of consumption, there are too many commas. The comma may be a humble-looking sort of a thing, but it does have a very important purpose (in fact, more than one), so treat it with respect.

The semi-colon

Don't forget semi-colons, either. You will notice throughout this book that semi-colons are used quite frequently in places where you could quite properly use a full stop; but because the following sentence is still dealing with a similar aspect of the same subject, and because too many full stops can make a letter feel very 'jumpy'; and because, most of all, you should never start a new sentence with 'but' or 'and', the semi-colon acts as a useful halfway house between a comma and a full stop – which, when you look at it, is precisely what it is!

The observant reader will look at that last sentence and say: 'But from time to time, in this book, a sentence *has* been started with "but" or "and".' Well, indeed, we confess you are right; but this is where a certain licence can come into books or dialogue which is inexcusable in business correspondence, and we discuss this aspect in more detail a little later on.

Of all the punctuation marks, the apostrophe is probably the most ill-used, perhaps because the rules governing it seem somewhat vague, though in fact they are very precise.

The apostrophe

An apostrophe is used at the end of a noun or a proper name to indicate something belonging to that person: 'The boss's office'; 'Mr Smith's pen'. (After a word ending in -ss the third 's' that would appear after the apostrophe is sometimes left out, e.g. 'the boss' office', but either form is equally correct.)

An apostrophe is also used to denote a missing letter: 'can't', 'doesn't', 'hasn't', 'haven't', 'won't', are all examples of the apostrophe standing in for the 'o' of 'not'. Be careful to put the apostrophe in the correct place – many people put it before the 'nt' (for example 'have'nt), making nonsense of the rule because it is not then replacing anything except the gap between 'have' and the non-existent word 'nt'. There is one anomaly in the list of examples, and that is 'won't'. There is, of course, no such word as 'wo' – the whole word being a contraction of the phrase 'will not', created because 'willn't' would be almost impossible to say. Watch out for the old-fashioned word 'wont', pronounced the same way and seldom used nowadays, but occasionally found in the phrase 'as is his wont', meaning 'as he usually does'.

Where the use of the apostrophe often gets muddled is with the pronoun 'it'. Here, and exceptionally, the apostrophe is *only* used to denote a missing part of another word, usually 'is' or 'has'; for example 'it's [it is] raining'; 'it's [it has] stopped raining'. You must *never* put an apostrophe with the pronoun to denote something belonging to it: 'the dog has *its* bone', *not* 'the dog has *it's* bone' – although, of course, you would write 'the *dog's* bone'.

The controversy (correctly pronounced *con*troversy, by the way, not con*tro*versy) about 'different from', 'different to' and 'different than' drags on; strictly speaking, 'different from' is correct in England, 'different than' in America; and many people use 'different to' all the time, particularly in speech. You may also find the Americanized spelling 'alright' used quite frequently nowadays, in place of the English form, 'all right'.

Business language naturally tends to be more formal than the sort of letter you would write to a friend, but that need not mean it should be pompous. If your boss is inclined to use four syllables where one will do (or, for that matter, four *words* where one will do) you could gently suggest simpler alternatives. It shouldn't be slangy, but there's no reason why it shouldn't be straightforward. For example:

> Dear Mr Smith,
> I am in receipt of your correspondence of the 21st instant in which you inform me that the order I have been awaiting since the 4th ultimo was due to be despatched by you last Monday, to arrive at these premises not later than Friday of the same week. I have to regretfully inform you that this order has still not been forthcoming and I would be grateful to now obtain your opinion as to what might have occurred to delay this matter still further.

This is a horrible letter; it is wordy and unclear and, what is worse, contains two split infinitives, a grammatical sin which we will deal with shortly. Also, to use words like 'instant' (to mean the present month) and 'ultimo' (last month) is terribly outdated, though certain people (the Mr Foggits of this world) cling to them. The letter would read much better thus:

> Dear Mr Smith,
> Thank you for your letter telling me that the order for which I have been waiting since the 4th of last month was due here not later than Friday of last week. Unfortunately it has still not arrived, and I should be glad of an explanation for this continuing delay.

Phrased this way, it still sounds business-like but much less pompous and for that reason, strangely, carries more weight. The writer of the first letter could be a waffly old fool fussing on; the writer of the second letter is a busy man whose patience is rapidly running out. Most importantly, however, the meaning is the same.

Always be very careful, when altering anything, that you do not change the sense. A point worth noting here is that, if you are working for a writer, you really should not change anything without consulting him first. Writers often break, or severely bend, grammatical rules in the interests of artistic licence (for example, starting sentences with 'but' or 'and'!); if a sentence sounds odd, they usually have a very good reason for *wanting* it to sound odd. It can cause unbounded fury and frustration if you start editing it back into 'good English'. (One secretary, whose author boss was writing a book about Gainsborough, the English artist, painstakingly edited all the direct quotes from Gainsborough's letters, 'correcting' the eighteenth-century grammar and spelling – she didn't last long!) By all means ask, 'Did you really mean to say that?', but don't go blithely ahead on your own initiative in this case.

Split infinitives

Which brings us neatly to the dreaded split infinitive. This is perhaps the most common of grammatical mistakes – we do it all the time in normal speech, and if your writer employer does it, *don't* change it without asking him first. But in business correspondence it is a glaring error and should always be corrected, though again your correction should be done with tact and with care not to alter the meaning. What is a split infinitive? A good example is the incomparable and beloved 'To boldly go where no man has gone before', which announced the opening of each 'Star Trek' episode. 'To go' is the infinitive of the verb, and no word should ever be allowed to break it up, no matter how 'bold' it may be.

If you look back at the first example letter in this chapter, on page 87, you will notice the two split infinitives: '. . . to regretfully inform you . . .' and '. . . to now obtain . . .'. There are several ways you could improve the first instance: 'Regretfully, I have to inform you . . .'; 'I have, regretfully, to inform you . . .'; 'I have to inform you regretfully . . .'. All are perfectly acceptable, though the last is perhaps the least elegant of the three. Note the position of the commas in the first two instances, lifting the word 'regretfully' slightly away from the main thrust of the sentence; in other words, 'I may regret doing it, but nevertheless *I have to inform you* that the order has not arrived.'

The second split infinitive is contained in a phrase so dreadful that there is really nothing to be done with it but re-phrase it completely, as has been done in the second example (see p. 87).

Hyphens and dashes

Hyphenating words must also be done carefully. You will probably have learnt, during your basic typing course, not to hyphenate the last words on consecutive lines, or the last word at the end of a page, but it is important also to break up a word in a logical place so that both halves of it are readable: for instance, divide 'readable' into 'read-able', but not 'rea-dable' or 'reada-ble'.

Here, it is worth touching on the use of the hyphen's big brother, the dash, which can also be a tricky animal. It can be used singly or in pairs, and normally indicates a pause. Used in pairs, dashes, like brackets or commas, mark off words which are not necessary to the meaning of the sentence; like commas, but unlike brackets (which can be used anywhere in a sentence, or even around an entire sentence), the pair of dashes may be used only in the middle of the sentence.

When used singly, the dash indicates an expectant or dramatic pause, introducing either clarification of the preceding remarks or a sudden and unexpected change of direction in a sentence. It is wonderfully effective used in this way, but don't overdo it. A sentence should not contain more than one 'dramatic' dash, as repetition can lead to confusion as to whether it is being used on its own or as one of a pair; and it can also make for very jumpy construction.

Correct addressing

Typing and shorthand lessons will have given you the basic information on how to lay out letters, but they may have missed

UBD/jse

Fantasy Manufacturing Co. Limited
48 Peter Pan Road
Wendyland
Somewhere.

30th October 1932

For the attention of J. Tinkerbell Esq.

Dear Sirs

We wrote to you in September about our new product range and, as to date we have heard nothing from you, felt we should contact you again.

Would you be kind enough to let us know whether you will be ordering further items from the new range.

We look forward to hearing from you.

Yours faithfully
CUSTOMADE FAIRYLAND LIMITED

C. Lamb
Director

some of the finer points of letter-writing, such as how to address people or firms, and the correct way of finishing off. Above and on the next page are samples of a letter, addressed correctly.

When you are writing to someone whose name you and your boss don't know, you must address him as 'Dear Sir', or, in the case of a letter written to a firm, without the designation of the person concerned, 'Dear Sirs' (this applies if you put 'for the attention of Mr X', too). At the end of a letter starting that way, you sign off 'Yours faithfully'. (Note that the 'f' of faithfully is in lower case, i.e. *not* a capital F – lots of people get that wrong, but *you* don't, naturally.)

A letter written to a firm is formal, and the company for whom you work is, in effect, writing the letter, even though your boss signs it. He does not write in the first person ('I', rather than 'we'). The above letter might also be addressed to the firm and sub-headed 'For the attention of the Purchasing Manager' if Mr Tinkerbell's name were unknown to you.

If you know the name of the person and write to 'Mr G. Smith', you address him as 'Dear Mr Smith', ending with 'Yours sincerely'.

```
yr. ref: JT/PT

Our ref: UBD/jse

J. Tinkerbell Esq.
Fantasy Manufacturing Co. Limited
48 Peter Pan Road
Wendyland
Somewhere.

                                        30th October 1932

Dear Mr Tinkerbell

I wrote to you in September about our new product range and,
as to date I have heard nothing from you, felt we should
contact you again.

Would you be kind enough to let me know whether you will be
ordering further items from the new range.

I look forward to hearing from you.

Yours sincerely




C. Lamb
Director
```

'Yours truly' is another way of ending, but only when in doubt, as one of the previous two endings should usually fit the bill.

The above letter is written on a personal basis to Mr Tinkerbell, so the Company name is not typed; Mr Lamb signs it but, as it is on headed Company paper, it is obviously a business letter. Addressing Mr Tinkerbell as 'Esq.' rather than 'Mr' is optional, but can be a nice, slightly old-fashioned touch. Many employers still prefer it, feeling that it adds a touch of 'class' or style.

Having dealt with your employer's appalling spelling and punctuation, sentence construction and addressing of correspondents, you must also ensure that the letter is well presented, clear and clean. 'Clean' may seem an odd word to use in the context of business correspondence, but we don't mean morally so; dark rub-out smudges, thumb-prints and creases do nothing for your image, and this applies as much to the carbon copies as to the top. You may think your carbons will lurk harmlessly in the files for ever, but remember that you may be asked to show one to someone important, and a revolting scrap of crumpled bank paper will not impress him, nor probably will he be able to read it. Don't be lazy about correcting your carbon copies – take out your mistake with Tippex paper or dab it carefully with correction fluid. You may have a self-correcting typewriter, in which case you will probably prefer to correct the copies afterwards, but in any case, don't neglect to do it.

If the mistake is too big to correct, or if by correcting it you have made the whole thing look worse, then the only solution is to start again. Don't get disheartened if a letter just *won't* go right even at the third or fourth attempt; some letters are like that, and it may be better to leave the beastly thing until last, by which time it may be in a better mood to allow itself to be typed properly.

Always make your correspondence look spacious, with well-matched margins and line-ends. This is not to say that you should begin every letter miles away from the letter-head and use sheets and sheets of paper; but even a long, complicated, close-packed letter with lots of sub-paragraphs won't look so daunting if it is spaced nicely. Don't forget, by the way, if your letter has to continue on to another page, to put the date, whom the letter is addressed to, and a shortened version of their address at the top of each continuation sheet. Should the pages become separated, you won't then be faced with a mysterious Page Two whose origins you have forgotten.

Whatever else you may feel about your office correspondence, or however you care to organize it, remember that it is nice to get a letter. English is a beautiful, diverse language – probably the most subtle of all the European tongues, with certainly one of the largest vocabularies – and even if your boss doesn't use it as such, you can make his correspondence look as though he does.

11 *Help! – Coping with a Crisis*

The essence of all crisis-coping is, of course, to keep calm. It would be impossible to enumerate all the crises which could arise in an office, but here are a few examples.

Your Boss Has Disappeared. This is probably *the* commonest, and some bosses are better at it than others. He will, however, almost invariably do it when the Very Important Visitor he didn't tell you was coming arrives; *or* when you thought he was safely at the Board meeting and the chairman rings in a towering rage because he isn't, and they can't start without him; *or* when the taxi to take him to the airport has just arrived, already twenty minutes late because of traffic, and is sitting clocking up the pennies while the seconds tick by towards take-off time.

Obviously the first thing to do is to *find him*, and here your Best Friends can help, if you work in a large company. Ask the telephone operator to ring round everyone she can think of to see if he is with them; get the post boy to help you scour the building and rout out the Gents' loos for you; in fact, possibly the best way is to get all your Best Friends on to his trail while you sit by the internal telephone waiting for a message to say that he's been found.

In the case of the Very Important Visitor, the first rule is to look as though you *were* expecting him. Sit him down comfortably with a cup of coffee and the paper, apologize for your boss being delayed 'in his previous meeting', and say you will just pop down to find out how long he will be – then send the search parties into action.

If you work in a 'one-girl/one-man' office you will not, of course, have the benefit of search parties, but in this case the likelihood will be that your boss has simply gone out and forgotten to come back. There is nothing whatever you can do, except to make yourself a cup of coffee as well and do your best to entertain the Very Important

Visitor (or the taxi driver) until either your boss turns up, or the V.I.V. gets bored and leaves.

The VIP Brings an Unexpected 'Guest'. This need not be too worrying if it is merely a question of an extra place at a restaurant table (though some maîtres can get quite ratty if you haven't given them the correct numbers); but if it involves tickets for the theatre, opera, Wimbledon or similar, it can be very nearly disastrous.

Don't gape in horror and gasp, 'But we've only got six tickets!' Make your way as quickly and unobtrusively as you can to the box office and have your hysterics there. Most box office staff are extremely helpful if you appeal to the hero in them. Explain your appallingly embarrassing situation, and they will almost certainly do all they can to help. Like hotels, theatres usually have one or two spare seats even for the most popular events; you may have to accept a single seat somewhere apart from the rest of your group, or *you* may have to plead a sudden migraine and miss the performance if there is absolutely no place to squeeze another body in. Don't take it too hard if it is the latter; if the VIP really *is* important, your boss will be so grateful to you for saving the day that he will surely make it up to you.

The Hotel Has Forgotten to Book the Room. This will happen to coincide with an international conference invading the town so that every hotel within a ten-mile radius is fully booked. Unless you forgot to write and confirm the booking, it is the hotel's fault (even then it is half their fault), so keep calm, talk to the manager and get him to sort it out. Don't shout and lose your temper – most hotels, even at peak times, keep one or two rooms or suites empty, and your boss might fortuitously end up in the penthouse suite if you are firm but pleasant; if you are not, he won't get anything at all.

If all else fails, your faithful travel agent might be able to help out, but don't count on this. It is better to tackle the hotel direct first of all.

You Have Lost a Vital File. If you really have lost it – and it is astonishing how often 'lost' files turn up under the boss's desk or in the back of his car – the only thing to do is be honest. In fact if you have truly forgotten, lost or neglected anything important (perish the thought!) honesty is the best policy. Don't try to hide the fact, make excuses or lay the blame anywhere else. We all make mistakes sometimes. Face the boss and apologize, simply and straightforwardly. Even the most irascible person finds it difficult to be enraged when confronted in this way, and the chances are he will be able to suggest some way to avert disaster.

There Is a Death in His Family. If, due to circumstances, you are the one who has to tell him (because he is away or at a meeting, say), try to get him somewhere private and tell him straight. There is no way to soften such a blow. Just say something like: 'Mr Smith, I'm afraid there is bad news. Your wife has just telephoned to say that your mother has died very suddenly. I am so sorry.' Then wait. It will take a few moments for the news to sink in. Shock sometimes encourages people to disbelieve bad news; he may ask all sorts of questions you cannot possibly answer like how, why, when, and so on. During those moments, don't bombard him with all the practical things you have thought of to help him, or force him to sit down, or thrust an unwanted cup of tea at him. It may help you to be terribly practical, but it will not help him to be bossed about. On the other hand, don't stand staring at him like a beached fish, waiting for instructions. It depends on your relationship with him whether you stay with him or leave him alone, but when you judge that he may be beginning to think more clearly, you can suggest one or two things he might find helpful: 'Would you like me to arrange for a taxi to take you home?' (He may say No – some people find the discipline of driving very therapeutic at moments of crisis.) 'Shall I explain to Mr Green why you can't be at the meeting this afternoon?' (Again, he may prefer to tell people himself.) 'Would it help if I collected the children from school?'

Whatever suggestions you can think of, make them short-term – he won't want to think about rearranging the following week's appointments, let alone the trip to Australia in a fortnight's time.

Whatever else, be guided by him. You will obviously answer his mail in his absence, and you may be involved in the arrangements over the funeral, funeral service sheets, flowers, notices to newspapers and so on. Make sure you are always easily get-at-able by him, even if there is not much actual work to do; this is a good moment to go through his personal documents that you hold, and familiarize yourself thoroughly with what is there (some of it may be pretty old, and even the most efficient secretary is not blessed with instant recall of matters that occurred several years ago), so that if he rings with a query about some obscure insurance policy that matured five years ago, you can have the answer ready. Stand, 'like a greyhound in the slips', prepared to do whatever he asks at a moment's notice; but don't flap about, constantly asking if there is anything you can do; and don't be officious. Let him ask – it will be much more helpful and less irritating for him in the long run.

The trouble with most crises, whether in life or in the office, is that, when it comes down to it, there is very little that you can physically *do* – one of the reasons for the displacement tea-making activity that we all know so well. The best you can do in nearly every crisis situation is be calm, and be *there*. Now is not the time to waft out and have a chat with your friend on the fourth floor, or take a long lunch-hour meandering round Marks & Spencer. If you do have to go out, let someone know where you are and how long you will be, or leave a message on the answerphone; if there is no message-taker and no answerphone, and it is a real crisis, you will just have to stick around, frustrating as that may be. It is a matter of loyalty, really, and that is what the next chapter is about.

12 *Attitude and Loyalty*

Do not be fooled – every successful secretary has a hard core of basic experience behind her. She has learned from the bottom rung, and only her hard-headed, realistic attitude, her willingness to work hard, her enthusiasm and loyalty have got her to the peak of her profession. There is no such thing as 'the easy way' – no one has success dropped gently into her lap without trying for it – so the best thing to do at the very beginning is tackle your mundane job with gusto.

If you are quick, accurate and positive, someone more senior will spot you and want you to work for him. If you sit about sighing and waiting for five o'clock, you will stay there for ever. Your mental attitude affects your physical wellbeing, too. Approach the typing of twelve hundred envelopes despondently, and they will take ages, you will make hundreds of mistakes, half of them will have to be typed again, your back and head will ache, and life generally will be a misery. Of course nobody enjoys doing a really grotty job, but you can make it worse by slouching about it.

Grumpiness breeds grumpiness, so if you are sullen and unwilling, the boss will slam the work on your desk and won't say 'Please'. At this point we should say that obviously office relationships are not only up to you. Some employers will always be cross and won't say 'Please', no matter how willing and bright you try to be. If you are working for one of these, then turn to page 13, consider Mr Foggit – and leave. Even as a beginner you do not have to work in a place where you are miserable and with people who are horrible to you, so find another job as soon as you can; but as you do, consider for a moment, with brutal honesty, whether your own attitude has not contributed even slightly to their poor treatment of you.

Taking an interest in every aspect of your job, no matter how trivial, is vitally important, especially to the senior secretary. You should, for example, read what you are typing and make sense of it, rather than treating it as a load of words flung down any-old-how. You may notice a mistake, or have heard something which could be relevant, in which case you should ask your boss about it. Your information may not be correct, but the fact that you have taken the trouble to notice will be appreciated.

When he is obviously feeling under the weather, ask if he would like a hot drink or an aspirin. If he has been away, or one of his children has taken an exam, or his wife is in hospital, ask him about it; not with deeply probing questions, or expecting the conversation to go on for hours, but quite simply, as one friendly human being to another.

Active interest in your work and your boss is the first step towards the total loyalty which is expected of the senior secretary. It is perhaps the only absolute, unshakeable, unbreakable rule in a secretary's life, and so important is it that it can be written thus:

> **You must always be one hundred per cent loyal to your boss whoever he is, and if for any reason you cannot be, then you should leave.**

There are no half-measures; in certain highly charged situations, such as company takeovers or internal political upheavals, you may be the only person in the office whom your boss can trust completely. Even in the ordinary day-to-day routine, he should feel that your loyalty is unquestioned. This does not mean you should be slavish; it is not disloyal to tell someone when you think they are wrong, even if saying it brings thunderbolts of rage raining down on your head. If he trusts you he will come round, when he has cooled down, to the fact that you were prompted by genuine concern, and he may even allow that you were right.

Your employer's firm comes first when it comes to loyalty. If it goes against the grain to lie that your boss is not there when he is, or to tell people, 'The cheque's in the post', when it patently obviously is not, then you need to find a job where you are, perhaps, a smaller cog in a larger wheel. Otherwise, compromise your morals about lying for the greater good of the firm, and become a realist; a well-organized office will not require too many lies of this sort, but there are always situations where a white lie will save embarrassment, and you have to learn to recognize and handle them.

Not all forms of loyalty involve compromises with morality; you should remember that you are on the same side as the firm which pays you. You work for the greater prosperity of your firm, and when your friend who works for the rival company down the street asks you what is going on, you must 'clam up'. No matter how sensational the current saga, *do not discuss it*. Be ignorant, or even bored ('Same old dull routine, nothing ever happens in our office!'), if it helps to put off probing questions, but, above all, be mum. (As we mentioned earlier, some firms have their staff bonded – that is to say, insurance cover is obtained after some sort of investigation has been carried out into the background and reliability of the staff.) You should be completely reliable and loyal, in any case, and never pass on anything, however intriguing, to someone outside your company.

Loyalty in an office between secretary and boss extends to people who work for the same firm. If your boss tells you something, whether to do with business or personal matters, about himself or someone else in the firm, *keep silent*. Discretion is *always* the better part of valour – or, in this case, chatter.

Only if your boss trusts you absolutely can your job become as completely fulfilling as a secretarial job can be. A top secretary works as part of a team *with* her boss, rather than as an underling *for* him; she is a sifter of information, an arranger, a correspondent, a confidante, friend, organizer, stand-in, bulwark against any slings or arrows that come his way. If all this sounds unbearably steadfast, there is another aspect which should be seriously considered: as a secretary there is nothing, absolutely *nothing*, which is 'not your job'. If his shoes need cleaning, you must be the shoe-shine boy; if he needs a stitch in time, you must be the needlewoman; if his office is a tip, you must be the charlady. (We have already mentioned that you should probably keep supplies of polishes for furniture, shoes, and possibly even silver, needles and thread and a good hangover cure.) Before you are put off for ever by visions of scrubbing and cleaning in between letters, let us say that these chores should not be your everyday lot. A secretary is expected to look well-groomed, and you should not be expected to wreck your nails and good clothes by constant requests to do the housework; but in an emergency, when he has stepped in a puddle and lost a button off his shirt and the chairman is coming to lunch, don't have any delusions about flouncing out with: '*I'm* not paid to clean his shoes' – you *are*!

13 *Promotion or Staying Put*

Promotion can simply be from one secretarial position to another, or from secretary to something else entirely – executive, salesperson, or any number of alternatives, including that exalted and mysterious person, the Personal Assistant, who is not at all like a secretary; later on, we will try to explain what sets her apart.

Obviously, the final choice is yours. You should not allow yourself to be dragged up by your boss, should he be promoted, if you feel that you would not be able, or want, to cope with his new responsibilities; equally, you should not allow yourself to be held back if an enticing opportunity comes your way. Think carefully, and examine your attitudes. It will not look good on your CV if you have moved from job to job too often. When you are just starting your career, to work loyally and well for someone for one or two years before making a change is quite reasonable – to change every six months or so looks a bit flighty (although, of course, if you are absolutely miserable, you don't have to slog through twelve months' hard labour before making the break). Your career, as it progresses, should show a natural curve of length of service, so that your first jobs probably last between one and two years each, gradually extending to longer service as you become more senior. This is not merely cosmetic; the more senior your job, the longer it takes to become fully integrated into it, to build up a relationship of mutual trust and respect between you and your employer.

As usual, there are advantages and disadvantages in equal proportion to being promoted or staying put. If, for instance, your boss is moving on, leaving you in the same job, you will be expected to take on his successor and will have the advantage of knowing the ropes better than your new boss. As long as you treat this situation tactfully, he will see it as an advantage, too, since he can use your experience to help settle himself in.

When you have done a job for some time, you get to know where corners can safely be cut, what can be left until tomorrow, or even next week – or, dare we say it, next year? (As long as you don't let it outgrow itself, a 'pending' basket is a useful thing, into which you put things you can't imagine what to do with but don't dare throw away. You nearly always find, after a year, that they can be chucked out with a clear conscience!) As a result there is less pressure on you, more time for your own life. You also stay with the camaraderie of your colleagues. Despite the notes on friendly office relationships, promotions can cause jealousies; as you move up, your greater responsibilities and the more confidential nature of your job will be bound to distance you from your old friends, and you may find that most damning of phrases, 'She's changed!', accompanied by a disapproving shake of the head, being muttered behind your newly promoted back.

Don't let that put you off promotion, of course; but bear in mind that, if you are promoted, you will be expected to give more of yourself to the job. No matter how exciting the prospects, no job is without its groundwork, and this monster is with you always. The less mundane a job is, the more the groundwork *must* be done efficiently, even though it appears to take a back seat. You will probably find that you are working late, not to entertain a visiting bigwig, but simply to catch up on your filing.

The bigger the wig you work for, the more the job will demand to come first in your life, and if you cannot, in all honesty, accept that premise, then you should remain contentedly where you are; but if you don't have too many personal commitments and are prepared to throw yourself wholeheartedly into the career of a personal, private, top-flight secretary, then the sky's the limit. A top secretary is worth her weight in platinum and can wield much influence and power, as well as reaping rewards, both financial and personal – and now is the time to talk about Personal Assistants.

Personal Secretaries

Some secretaries nowadays call themselves personal assistants in self-defence as much as anything, to distinguish themselves from the shorthand typists who are calling themselves secretaries. In fact, a true Personal Assistant is not a glorified secretary but a comparatively rare creature, found only in rather exalted places. Royalty has Personal Assistants (although, just to be perverse, they call them Private Secretaries) and they are generally men; the same applies to members of the Cabinet (here they are Cabinet Secretaries, or Principal Private Secretaries), to Ambassadors, and sometimes to the chairmen or senior executives of very large commercial conglomerates.

As one of these exotic creatures you would do very little typing or filing – only certain very confidential correspondence, or your employer's most private and personal letters – the day-to-day items being dealt with by a junior secretary, or even by several of them. If this sounds too appealing for words, there is, of course, a price to be paid. In return for being relieved of the workaday life, you look after all aspects of your boss's business, social and private life. You protect him, plan for him, organize, stand in for him when necessary, attend meetings with and for him, think about him and for him twenty-four hours a day. You are his right hand, his left hand, his *alter ego*. You are very unlikely to have much time for a life of your own; the demands of the job do not make allowances for attending your child's Nativity play, or idyllic romantic weekends with a boyfriend; but there are many rewards. You will probably have a car, and a dress allowance. You may travel. You will go to receptions, banquets, Royal or Parliamentary functions either with him or in his place. You will be entrusted with matters of the utmost confidentiality and, as a result, will be isolated, as much as your ivory-towered boss, from the normal helter-skelter of everyday office life.

It is one of the most involving, fascinating jobs in the world, and probably one of the loneliest.

14 'Horses for Courses' – Specialist Skills

From time to time, you will see advertisements for secretarial jobs which seem to need some kind of specialist knowledge: 'Medical Secretaries', 'Legal Secretaries' and so on. There are also those which state that a foreign language would be an asset.

Legal Secretaries

The Association of Legal Secretaries, established in 1976, sets examinations to gain the Legal Secretaries Certificate and the Legal Secretaries Diploma, the latter being the higher level. Either can qualify you to become a Licentiate Member or an Associate Member and, given the necessary experience and position, it is possible to go on and become a Fellow. They have a comprehensive list of colleges and polytechnics countrywide which offer A.L.S. courses; should you happen to find yourself in Malaysia or Nigeria and want to become a Legal Secretary, they have courses there, too! Their address and telephone number are given at the end of this book; if you send them a stamped self-addressed envelope, they will let you have full details of courses, colleges where you can pursue them, the examinations and what they entail, as well as a brief history of the Association to the present date.

There is also now an Institute of Legal Secretaries, based in London, which has been in operation for only a couple of years but offers the possibility of similar exams and qualifications. The Law Society, however, is more favourably inclined towards the Association.

Medical Secretaries

It is not essential to have a medical secretarial training to become a medical secretary, although an interest in the subject may mean you have glanced at Gray's *Anatomy* or Grant's *Atlas* at some time. In some medical jobs it helps if you are not too squeamish! You must be good at spelling and a very accurate typist, as chemical formulae, enzyme or drug descriptions can sometimes mean something quite different merely by the alteration of a single letter. Intelligence and a strong desire to produce careful, accurate work are vital to cope with the not inconsiderable technical jargon involved with medical work; although you may write the longer words out at first, you will probably devise your own outlines as you go on, so accurate shorthand is a must. In a research laboratory you may be asked to produce diagrams of chemical structures from the doctors' rough sketches.

There are courses for those wishing to become fully trained medical secretaries, one of which can be followed at the Hammersmith and West London College in Barons Court, London W14. The course is of two years' duration and entry requirements are currently at least four passes at 'O' level or equivalent, unless you have trained as a nurse (State-Enrolled, or Nursing Auxiliary) when one 'O'-level pass will suffice for entry. They also accept mature students on the course.

All aspects of secretarial training are covered, with particular emphasis on the medical side, including the National Health Service and the social services. Medical secretaries might also like to contact the Association of Medical Secretaries, which will give details of examination syllabuses.

Languages

Jobs with foreign languages are scarce. This is true even now, in these days of the Common Market and 'international understanding' – there is still a marked lack of such understanding in the average British office. Much international correspondence is carried on in English, and jobs which require knowledge of a foreign language (most likely to be in banks in the City, where the work content might not be all that exciting) generally use the foreign language for only about thirty per cent of the time. Your best chance of using your foreign language is if you develop a good knowledge of some particular subject, possibly of a technical nature; a degree in chemical engineering would probably ensure plenty of work translating documents into English (you should only expect to be paid for translating *into* your own language, not into the foreign language). There is a good chance, too, of obtaining work as an interpreter if your foreign language is absolutely perfect and you speak two (or more) languages as if they were your own. You have to be a very quick thinker for that sort of work, and have strong nerves, as much interpreting work is for international conferences, frequently on technical subjects.

From the secretarial angle, regard your language knowledge as an asset, use it at every opportunity, but don't expect to be able to earn a living just on the fact of knowing a foreign language. Bone up on something really technical, learn shorthand in it (Pitman have little books to help you adapt your English shorthand to other languages), and keep your secretarial skills absolutely up to scratch in English. You may then find that you decide to work abroad, where your English will be your greatest asset, and your knowledge of a specialized topic, plus shorthand in whatever languages you know, will be of the greatest use.

One way in which a language or two may come in useful is at conferences, simply in your capacity as general factotum, where a foreign delegate may approach you and ask what time the last bus goes to Heathrow, or will need help in booking his flight back to Paris, Madrid, Munich or wherever. A smile and a few sentences in his own language will go far, while at the same time you are telling him about the buses or booking his seat on the plane for him.

A secretary who is fluent in a foreign language can be asked to help out when an interpreter is unavailable (or when the firm doesn't want to pay the high rates that qualified interpreters can demand for their services), and then you may well find yourself in the boardroom interpreting over a gourmet lunch – being expected to translate: '. . . and it was the most amazing putt, only an inch from the hole, and it should have gone down when suddenly up popped this mole . . .'

The most unlikely situations happen to secretaries at some time or other!

You may be asked to meet an overseas visitor at the airport if your boss is involved with something equally important at the time. Your driving skills (and your strong arms, if you have to help carry the baggage) must be on form; and if the visitor doesn't speak English, your language ability and knowledge of Britain will be tested, too, as a visitor, on arrival, always expects a native to know all the answers to all the questions he has about Britain and the sights you see en route to his hotel.

A lot of secretarial jobs will advertise a requirement for a foreign language, but most often they will have *up to* (seldom more than) a thirty per cent foreign-language content in the job. The occasional employer will own up, but many try and tempt secretaries with the language part, and then the poor girl finds out, too late, that the job, though possibly interesting, is not quite what she was hoping for. This applies very often in England, but happily is not exclusively so; there are real jobs which need *all* your skills, including your language knowledge, just in running the office. Perhaps they have a Paris office with whom they communicate all the time, resulting in a constant use of French, both written and spoken. Perhaps they deal with Spain, and telephone calls (when you can get through) are mostly in Spanish, while all correspondence is in Spanish with copies in English for the files at the British end.

Don't lose hope, but don't expect a much higher salary for knowing the language *per se*. There is a much better chance of earning a higher salary if you are *so* good at the job – and do it better than anyone else ever has – that you make yourself *almost* (no one ever is quite) indispensable.

15 *Agencies*

Secretarial agencies are many and varied; one of the rather irritating things you will probably find about them is that the advertised job which attracts you to the agency in the first place has inevitably 'just gone' when you go and see them. Not to say that the actual job wasn't available at the time they advertised it, but as it *was* their plum job, it did go instantly – and since they naturally need more people all the time, they were delighted to be able to advertise such an attractive position. You may feel fed up with this sort of thing but, to be realistic, the agency is hardly likely to advertise its least attractive job, and only one person is needed to fill each vacancy.

Of course, you can also find yourself a job in the newspaper columns (the *Times* 'Crème de la Crème' on Wednesdays and Thursdays, and the *Guardian* on Mondays, for example), since many companies like to advertise their job vacancies without having to pay agency fees.

If you are in the position of trying to find someone for your firm (or to replace you), unless you want every agency in town on the telephone to you offering a 'super girl', it is sensible to put the words 'no agencies' into your advertisements. Advertising is cheaper, but more time-consuming. You have to be around to interview all the applicants (even waiting for those who don't bother to keep the appointment), and you may have to weed out the useless ones – a job which the agency could do for you. Agencies are naturally concerned with making a living; but the best are helpful and conscientious, and will try to send the most suitable person for the job.

Your application interview with an agency should go along much the same lines as an interview for a specific job, except that you may have to be slightly (even!) more honest. A well-presented CV is a must, and you should be prepared to answer fairly detailed questions about your personal life (for example, if you have recently married are you likely to have children? Soon? If not, why not?), and to allow yourself to be cross-examined about your experience, the type of personality you are, the sort of job you want (not as obvious as it seems) and the sort of boss you are most likely to get on with.

Your training may come under scrutiny, and most agencies who value their reputations will insist on testing your formal skills (don't stand on your dignity about tests, just because you *know* you are good – they really should test you), and not only on your shorthand and typing but probably your spelling and knowledge of English, and possibly your numeracy, too.

References will, or should, feature, even if the agency itself does not take them up; employers will certainly expect you to provide references.

An agency will usually give you some sort of letter of introduction to a potential employer, probably setting out the likely salary. Don't allow a new employer to talk you into accepting an apparently lower salary than offered, in order to pay a lower fee to the agency, and then increasing the salary to you later. Your agency is probably working quite hard on your behalf and you owe them some loyalty for finding you the job, if nothing else – apart from the fact that the agency's Terms of Business are probably being broken, which could result in your new employer being taken to court by them! Consider, too, if your future employer suggests such a thing, whether you want to start off on that footing, and whether you are going to be happy working with a boss who can do that to another business contact.

An agency should go to quite a lot of effort to find you the right job, and to fit the new secretary to the boss, so do try and tell the interviewer as much as you can about the sort of person you like to work with, and the sort of person you are.

Temporary Work

Temporary work can be very useful while you are looking for a permanent job, and there are agencies who treat you as if you were a permanent employee anyway, offering holidays and sickness benefit to full-time workers. Working for one of these can be much like being in a permanent job, except that you are still going from one firm to another for a short time.

Generally, a good 'temp' is not someone who has just qualified in shorthand and typing, or recently finished her training. Some years of experience in varied office situations make the best temporary filler-in secretaries, and there are some high positions where temporary people are needed who have a high level of expertise – such as the job where *you* may end up, working for the chairman or a senior director of a group of companies – where the permanent, and very valued, secretary is indisposed for long enough for it to be considered expedient to replace her with a temporary. Not all 'temps' are young girls with poor skills who don't care about their work – though some are, regrettably; if you can be the exception, you will be an invaluable asset to your agency and should be remunerated accordingly.

Try not to fuss about which part of town you work in – if you are serious about wanting work, you should be willing to go where you are sent. It is more acceptable for an older person, perhaps with children to meet from school and working short hours, to stipulate distance to and from work than it is for a full-time secretary.

There are agencies who specialize in older, more experienced people, and there are those who will send out *anyone anywhere* – 'bottoms on seats' seems to be their motto, and there can be a touch of the impersonal about them, since the girls who work in such agencies are often on commission and want to make as many placements as possible, sometimes regardless of the suitability of applicant to job or vice versa. If you are unhappy with one agency, there are plenty of others to choose from – for one or two individual recommendations, see the end of the book.

An agency has to make the usual deductions from pay for its employees, even the self-employed, although the genuinely free-lance can pay their own *tax* as long as the agency can be sure that the Inland Revenue is protected – it is the agency's responsibility to collect tax and national insurance, and even the self-employed have to have national insurance deductions made from their earnings through an agency. The only exceptions are for work which is considered by the DHSS to be unsupervisable, such as translation, interpreting, or home-based work.

Home Typing/Word Processing

Agency work can sometimes mean typing at home, or word processing. If you become unable to handle an office job, or grow tired of it, there is a good chance that you will be able to set up your own home typing group, if you are a really competent secretary; not necessarily an agency proper (you may be infringing some agency laws if you send people out to jobs), but possibly offering a service to, say, the legal profession, accountants or universities, providing first-class typing or word processing.

You will be involved in a certain amount of selling, of course, to ensure that you have a good flow of work, and you must be an absolutely first-class typist – and so should anyone who works with you. By its nature, selling means that you can't actually be typing all the time, or even be at home by the telephone, so be certain that there is someone competent to take a message for you when you are out, and possibly able to handle any work which is on hand, too. You will need to be a fairly good judge of typing standard when choosing someone to help you, and you must hope that that person will be as enthusiastic as you are when dealing with clients.

Working in an Agency

You may begin to think that you could actually work in an agency yourself. There is no particular mystique about it – it is necessary, as in all office jobs, to use common sense, be meticulous about planning, organizing and paperwork (writing everything down bores some people), and to like people – not just nice people, of course, or good staff. Sometimes people come in whom you can't use – people with BO (sorry to bring that up again!) or someone with the kind of story that makes it hard for you to keep a straight face (like the lady who can only work in the afternoons because in the mornings she has trouble with 'wind', and she must have an office to herself because it can be 'awkward' for others to have to share with her! – we're not making this up).

Agency work involves dealing with the same kind of people that you would meet everywhere; but whereas by working in a one-secretary/one-boss situation you get used to everything, all the running of the office and the people, the company product(s) and so on (and your very own boss), in an agency you will probably handle a greater variety of people and possibly learn a little about many more companies and their products and services, as well as learning to handle delicate situations between people – such as the newly placed (by you) secretary who isn't at all sure she wants to stay with an apparently impossible boss. You may be able either to persuade her to stay and give him another try, or to coax him into showing her his pleasanter, more tolerant side. The practice of diplomacy comes into play just as often as it would if you were the secretary dealing with the apparently intractable boss.

If you move from temporary yourself to agency 'temp' controller, try to remember how it felt when you were on the receiving end of the boring jobs – and the wages that went with them! Remember that each employee wants to be regarded as an individual and to have her own wishes taken into account; also that the employer's word on a temporary must be considered – even when you *know* he is impossible. He may, nevertheless, be right that her skills are lousy! You must use only the best person for the job.

16 *The Future*

It may seem fatuous to suggest to the aspiring secretary just embarking on her career that one day she may give it all up and then, later in life, want to return to it again; but many women *do* have a very satisfying career prior to marriage, work part-time while their children are small, and later go back to work on a full-time, or nearly full-time, basis. It is best to acquire the highest possible level of skills, and to keep them in peak condition.

The more you have developed your skills (including, say, shorthand in a foreign language) and abilities on various sorts of typewriter, word processor, computer, telex, switchboard, etc., the more likely you are to be able to return to work in later life and pick up the threads again. And it becomes ever more likely that women who have given up work for a time to look after their families will go back to the working world as soon as their children are felt to be off their hands. Work is always available for competent people in the secretarial field – it is one of the jobs which is needed throughout business, whatever area a company is engaged in. If you can offer a high standard of work, either on your own or with a group of other well-trained secretaries, you will almost always find that you are kept busy.

The aspiring secretary, though, would do well to remember that her skills are her fortune, and so keep them polished. Most employers prefer accurate to very speedy typing, as having to send letters back to the typist for correction is costly in firm's time. Far better to employ a more accurate typist, even if she is slightly slower. Shorthand should be written correctly, always, not just so that you can read it (that goes without saying), but also because the practice will help you to become faster and more efficient – *and* because, should you fall under a bus on the way home, someone else will be able to make head or tail of your shorthand notes.

The young secretary, although trained and (having read this book) well equipped to handle almost any secretarial job, should bear in mind that youth itself is a factor in how much progress she can make. With the additional experience she acquires with the years she will make an ever-improving secretary, but she will need to plod through the tedious part first. She can do a lot worse than be a junior secretary under the wing of someone older and more experienced. There is usually a good chance that if the older secretary leaves, the younger one can step into her shoes, principally because she already 'knows the ropes' . . . somewhat like the understudy getting the starring role when the leading lady falls sick!

Opportunities are everywhere for the really good secretary who has the right attitude, a willingness to learn and who takes pride in her work and her skills.

17 The 'Pending' File

In any office there are always those things that you know should not be thrown away, but somehow there just doesn't seem to be a logical place to put them, so they tend to sit in the 'Pending' file/basket/tray until either someone asks about them or you discover they have been there so long that they can now safely be filed under 'General' and forgotten about! (The 'Pending' file, incidentally, should *never* be the repository for all the filing you can't be bothered to do!)

The items in this chapter are rather like that. They are important but don't quite fit into any of the preceding chapters, so we have given them a section all to themselves. The first item might be handy to show your employer one day when he is in a mellow mood!

How To Be A Good Boss

The following are a few hints which many bosses would do well to heed. Most secretaries will function better as a result.

1. Remember your secretary's name.
2. Don't complain when your secretary is late occasionally, until you have found out the cause – she may have had a family crisis.
3. Provide a comfortable chair, a large enough desk, and her own telephone.
4. Tell her what you want (how you like your letters signed, how many copies, etc.). Don't hope that she will guess – she probably will, once she gets to know you – but don't expect it at the start.
5. Let her know how she is to handle calls, and how you like your telephone answered.
6. Give her responsibilities – like research, dealing with visitors, ordering equipment.

7. When you dictate, try and decide in advance what you are going to say – that way you won't waste her (paid) time and yours while you think in her presence – and her notebook won't be full of crossings-out where you've changed your mind twenty times in a sentence.
8. When using an audio machine, make sure it is switched on before you start speaking, and dictate clearly. It is not necessary to dictate every comma and full stop, but if your secretary would *prefer* you to dictate all punctuation (in a long document, the typing can become very fast and the dictation merely a sound in the ear which the fingers, not the brain, interpret) then specify *everything*.
9. When using audio, speak all proper names clearly, and *spell* them unless they are well known to her.
10. Still on audio, stipulate any extra copies *before* you start dictating the main body of the document; most secretaries don't listen right through a tape from beginning to end before starting work on it, as it is terribly time-wasting.
11. Keep your handwriting at least half-legible – your secretary will get through your work more quickly if she can read it.
12. Let your secretary sign some letters on your behalf (especially in your absence), and let her answer some letters herself. There is a good chance that her English is better than yours anyway when it comes to letter-writing!
13. Let your secretary get involved in your business; introduce her to people, so she will be able to deal with them for you when you are otherwise engaged; if you treat her simply as a shorthand typist/coffee-maker, she will lose interest and become just that.
14. Try asking the switchboard to get your calls if you haven't time to dial them yourself or the number is constantly engaged – it is a waste of your secretary's time when she could be doing something more interesting and productive.
15. Keep your office equipment up to date. Secretaries can't produce first-class work on second-class machinery. But leave her to choose her typewriter.

16. The filing system, although in existence for your benefit, is often the exclusive territory of the secretary. Try and learn how to use it – not just for the purpose of saving your secretary work, but to save yourself time. Although your wish is basically her command, she may be deeply involved in something urgent at the very moment when you need a file equally urgently. Ask your secretary to provide you with a guide to the filing system, and use it.
17. Try not to keep secrets from your secretary – the very word 'secretary' is meant to imply that she is able to guard your secrets from the rest of the world – and she will if you confide in her.
18. One of the most annoying ways of keeping secrets from her is by putting something in your own diary and not letting her know. You probably insist that she checks with you before making appointments for you – so check with her before you make any.
19. Make time somewhere during the day for a little chat with her, even if it's only for ten minutes – to discuss diaries, future plans, papers for meetings, office gossip, personal problems (yours or hers). That way, the two of you will make a better team.
20. If there is someone to run errands, don't use your secretary – she may be doing something important for your business, even when she isn't actually typing, and *your* time is thus being wasted. You could, perhaps, buy your own cigars?
21. If your secretary is truly valuable, which presumably she must be:
    (a) tell her
    (b) give your work to her and no one else (who else could you trust to do it properly anyway?)
    (c) make sure she is well remunerated – a rise is a very good way of making someone feel appreciated
    (d) take her out to business lunches, exhibitions, etc., from time to time
    (e) only tell her off if it's vital – and never in front of anyone else (and don't tell anyone else off in front of

her, she'll be embarrassed unnecessarily and think less of you).

Creditors/Debtors

Just to state what may not always be obvious: creditors are people to whom you, or your firm, owe money; debtors are people who owe you money. Creditors start off being called suppliers, and only become creditors when they have sent their invoice and you haven't paid it. Debtors start off as customers or clients, and become debtors when *they* haven't paid.

If you are in charge of the bookkeeping, even if the figures are small, you still have to keep track of the debtors – and make them pay! Don't be squeamish about this – remember that the money they owe is vital to the survival of your firm – and your job!

Grievances

The time comes in the most well-ordered office when the secretary, in spite of her own best endeavours, feels aggrieved. Read your contract of employment – it should tell you whom you should complain to on an official basis; perhaps the personnel or office manager, if there is one, or possibly the Company Secretary. If you have a definite grievance and feel, day by day, that things are not getting better, don't bottle it up. It may be that your boss never says 'Good morning' or that your typewriter, which looked so beautiful, is an absolute pain to use and you are fed up with its foibles.

As far as the typewriter is concerned, call the mechanic and moan at him. But as regards the boss, if it really *is* something fairly trivial, try mentioning it to him. He probably hasn't given it a thought; perhaps he's already been in the office for an hour in the morning before you and therefore doesn't feel 'early-morningish' by the time you arrive (even if you are early, and you yourself start before the rest of the office staff). Not all bosses are angels, but most can be trained; and expressing your grievances, as long as they are not too many or too frequent, is the most likely way to lead to a better relationship between you.

If your unexpressed grievance is to do with a cold office, or the lack of lunch day after day, or having to walk up four flights of stairs *again* as the lift wasn't working, then it really should be expressed; you can almost certainly arrange for the office to be heated yourself. The lunch arrangements can be handled by ordering sandwiches in advance from a local sandwich/office-lunch supplier, to be delivered at a prearranged time (and almost certainly charged to the firm). The lift can be a bit more difficult. If it is old and decrepit and the building is, too (and so will you be, you feel, if you go on climbing those stairs, day after day), then you may have to discuss with your boss (or the company accountant) the possibility of either changing the maintenance arrangements for the lift or even having a new one installed – a major capital expense which your firm may not wish, or be unable, to go to.

Be straightforward about your grievance, and don't whinge. State what is wrong politely but firmly. Maybe nothing can be done about it, but at least you will probably feel better for having had your say – and then forget it and get on with your job.

Insurance Claims

When your boss has a tiny bump in his car – *not* his fault, of course – or when an employee of the firm makes a claim on the firm's insurance cover, a claim form will have to be completed. The insurance company will probably have supplied your office with claim forms, or you may have to telephone them to send one.

Most likely it will be your job to drag out of your boss the necessary information and detail concerning the incident, and then complete the form. Remember to keep a copy of everything before you send it off as, if a Court hearing is the result, you will need to bring your boss up to date with the details again just beforehand, as the hearing will almost certainly be months later.

Insurance matters in business are often best dealt with by referring to a solicitor for advice. A large firm may have its own legal department to deal with such matters; in any case, insurance in general is unlikely to be handled by a secretary without the assistance of professional advice.

Choosing a typewriter

You may have been trained recently, and therefore have possibly only ever used an electric typewriter. Perhaps you were trained to type twenty or more years ago and used a manual typewriter as a matter of course for years. Perhaps you have had experience only on an electronic, or even on a word processor. Whatever your experience, choosing a typewriter will be coloured by your preference, and the salesman will have an easier or tougher time with you if he is trying to sell you something about which you have no experience.

Make him demonstrate it and ask as many questions as you need, as often as you need to. Get him to leave the machine for you to try out for a few days – and get a lot of different ones on approval. Your employer will get his typing done, albeit with a different type-style from last week's, and he won't have to pay for a new machine until you are *sure*.

In Part Two we go into this matter in greater detail, especially about word processors, but there are certain things to bear in mind when you have the final choice about which typewriter to buy.

(i) Has it a comfortable keyboard?

(ii) Has it all the facilities you are looking for? Make a list, based on the following.

will it:

- embolden
- justify the right-hand margin
- store text
- centre automatically

Does it have:

- a screen or line display (if electronic)
- decimal tab (a boon when typing accounts)
- adjustable pitches (10, 12, 15 to the inch, at least)
- automatic, or easy, self-correction of errors

proportional spacing
foreign language accents, if required

(iii) Is it quiet enough in operation?

(iv) If other people are to use it, or if you are buying a number for the office, is it relatively easy to learn to use?

(v) What is the cost of maintenance, ribbons, new golf-balls/daisywheels, self-correcting tapes?

(vi) How quickly (*truthfully*) will the service engineer come to your aid?

Usually it is best to arrange a maintenance agreement for the repair of your typewriter(s). It is no help to contact a service engineer when something has gone wrong, only to be told that they will be with you in a couple of days – you need them *now*, and it is the maintenance contract customers who get the quickest service. Be sure you keep a note of the maintenance firm's telephone number (put a sticker on the machine itslf, so you can't lose it) and also the date when they last serviced it and when the next service visit is due. They should be willing to come to your aid during the maintenance year, whenever you contact them.

Keep the instruction manual for the new typewriter somewhere really handy – if it is electronic there will be lots of new tricks you can play with it, and you will probably not remember them all initially. Also make sure you have an adequate supply of the specific ribbons and correcting tapes it needs (if it is a self-correcting machine which most are these days). Check the price of these care fully; there are many sources of supply, even though the manufacturers keep bringing out machines which take only one particular ribbon, to try and ward off the competition. The competition is up to all the tricks, and you can certainly buy from it if you know where it is . . . and the competition will make itself known to you, never fear. If you don't actively discourage 'selling' telephone calls, you will have the salesmen on to you in no time and, quite honestly, you *are* after all on the side of saving your firm money, so you may well buy from people other than the official suppliers of the 'right' ribbon for your typewriter if the price is very much less.

Watch the quality, though; not all the cheaper alternatives are as good and you may find the ribbons are not as long as on the 'official' spools. At the same time, if you are perfectly happy with a copy which is a lot cheaper, even though not *quite* up to the correct standard, don't let the 'official' suppliers try to deter you.

When you have bought your new machine, don't lose track of the old one. Keep it in a cupboard somewhere for emergency use. Some of the old electrics are very heavy and are less worth keeping than the old manuals, but since you could perhaps be replacing a 'golfball' typewriter, that would certainly be well worth keeping somewhere. Don't let your boss decide that it has to be sold off – unless *you* want to buy it at the extraordinarily discounted low price for which the company could probably sell it to you!

Tips for 'temps'

A few points which, on arriving at a new job, you may find it is a good idea to go over with the employer.

1 *Style of letters, etc.*

(a) Are references to be included – where do they go?
(b) (i) Do you like your signature to be typed? (What is your name!) (ii) How do you like your signature to be typed – and what is your designation? (iii) Do you like the Company name to be typed?
(c) Do you like your paragraphs indented?
(d) When enclosures are indicated, do you want 'encs.' to go on letter?
(e) How many carbon copies?
(f) What colour flimsies?
(g) Can I have a sample of layout, please?

2 *Office procedure*

(a) How do you like your telephone answered (whether switchboard or office telephone)?
(b) When do you like tea/coffee? Are visitors to be offered? Is there a kitchen?

(c) Who's responsible for post at the end of the day?

3 *General*

(a) Take your own shorthand book/pencils/Tippex/dictionary.
(b) Ask where office machinery (photocopier, etc.) is located.
(c) Ask where the 'cloakroom' is (there's never anyone around to ask when you need to go).

. . . And tips for 'perms' too:

(a) Remember to make notes in your diary, not only for times of meetings, but also for general information, e.g. when important phone calls were made or received, telexes sent. It is also a good idea for planning ahead – noting down the date to follow up a certain item, etc. – even if you use a carry-forward file.
(b) It is very useful to keep old diaries and notepads. Sometimes a note jotted down which may not seem very important at the time can be valuable at a later date – and you can back-check how often the typewriter needed a visit from the repair man last year.
(c) If your boss goes out for a day or two, try to encourage him to phone in once or twice a day – especially if he is motoring around and is not at the number he should already have given you!
(d) Ask the switchboard to announce all calls before they're put through to you. It gives you the chance to dig out the relevant information first – or to think of an excuse not to talk to them, if necessary.
(e) Make sure all calls are returned as soon as possible.
(f) Make lists of everything you may need, e.g. telephone numbers most used, restaurants, hotels, meetings, names of head waiters, food your boss dislikes . . .
(g) Date all pieces of paper used for messages, no matter how

small. When found in a file, it will help to know the date – even if you can't remember the event!

(h) When you have finished a piece of work, make sure that you cross it through in your shorthand pad – or erase it from a tape if used. It can be very confusing to come across the odd few words that don't seem to belong – and worse, if they *do* seem to belong to your last piece of work, when they don't!

(i) Use plastic-covered paperclips for temporarily holding pieces of paper together, not metal. Metal makes nasty marks.

(j) Never let a paperclip get into the filing – something from another file will get stuck to the back, and you will have lost it for ever – until you want the paperclipped item, when you will cry 'Eureka' (possibly having previously cried buckets) over the lost one.

(k) You can staple something to the wall by treating your stapler as a staple-gun – keep it open and bang it where the staple emerges – if your wall is receptive you will have attached your paper to it.

(k) It is cheaper, in time at least, to use window envelopes than to type an envelope to go with every letter – and this applies too to those produced on a word processor or an electronic typewriter. But remember to make sure that the address on the letter appears in the right place to show through the window, otherwise you may have to fold and then refold your correspondence, which looks inefficient and untidy. Printers can place tiny marks strategically to indicate the place to type the address on headed paper, if asked.

(l) You don't have to throw away paper which has been used on one side, if what was on it and is no longer needed is not confidential; use it as scrap.

(m) Get a large diary that you can see at a glance from across the room – it doesn't have to be pretty, just functional. Also a clock – same applies (but don't watch it!).

(n) Keep a handy list of numbers of odd useful people – the doctor, the printer, the typewriter repair man, the garage

– on the wall, if it doesn't make your office look too messy.

(o) Keep a captive pen or pencil chained to your desk, so that if all the others escape, at least one can't be made off with.

(p) Keep spare keys to almost everything somewhere safe (at home, perhaps, but not without asking your employer's permission).

(q) Make sure you know the different weights of paper: Bank equals flimsy (used for carbon copies, mostly); bond may have several weights: 100 gm^2 and 85 gm^2 are the most usual. Take care not to confuse different weights of paper and differing textures; 'laid' and 'wove' are frequently occurring names. Laid paper has a lined, textured surface; 'Conqueror' is a well-known make of laid paper. 'Conqueror' also make wove, a flat-surfaced good-quality paper. Ordinary bond, similar to 'wove', is made by Croxley and other paper merchants.

Paper also can be different *shades* of white (Croxley is generally slightly greyish). So – don't mix them up.

18 Major Conferences and Seminars

You may find yourself in a central position when a large-scale conference is to be organized. This can be the real fun part of the job, as you will probably have to contact speakers, visit several venues in order to choose one, speak to banqueting departments about menus, numbers and facilities, book interpreters and/or translators (if it is an international conference) and recording technicians, arrange for overhead projectors, flip charts, etc., to be provided, as well as handling all the printing and despatch of invitations to delegates, and their responses. You may be asked to arrange for a video to be made before the conference, either of products or to demonstrate the potential of, say, a part of the country for development, or an exhibition hall for future exhibitions, or possibly of the conference itself. There may be evening social events to plan, dinners with or without spouses (many delegates are female, so do not refer to their 'wives'), theatre tickets for 300, coaches to book to transport them, day outings on the river with boats to be chartered, days at Windsor, the races, tennis or cricket, shopping trips for the spouses (!) and possibly individual interpreters where there are important side meetings between two or three delegates.

A large international conference may take two or more years of organization; you are not likely to be expected to handle such a conference on your own in your secretarial capacity. You would have to devote all your time, and more, just to this task, and your boss would certainly not get his letters typed by *you* for a while!

It has been suggested by professional conference organizers* that, during the planning and run-up to a major conference, the organizer in a company (that is, *you*), in the case where no professional organizer is employed, may be involved in something like:

* See Geoffrey V. Smith, *Good Conference Management*, The Conference Checklist' (British Tourist Authority), and other related publications from the BTA.

1000 telephone calls – incoming and outgoing

750 letters – all to be signed

150 telexes

65 contracts to be drawn up and signed, etc.

50 extra staff to be employed

whereas, by using a professional organizing firm, you could (with luck) be involved in a few telephone calls only, leaving the bulk of the organizing to them – all your company has to do is to foot the bill. Many firms, particularly trade associations, international societies and firms with a technical side and new discoveries to be fully explained to large numbers of people, do in fact use professional organizers, and there is almost no alternative if you are planning a big meeting.

You will find you are not out of a job though, since you will be the 'link-man' and your position will probably be to make many of the decisions which the organizers will ask for over the planning months ahead.

It is necessary to be clear, when beginning the organization of a conference, just what its objectives are; for example, some gatherings are expected to pay for themselves and, indeed, make a profit for the firm; some are a form of public relations exercise, where invitees come to see what your firm is selling, and your firm's outlay on the cost of the conference is not recouped in delegates' fees. Sometimes your firm will acquire a sponsor (for example, a drugs manufacturer might sponsor a medical conference) – and you may have to find a sponsor for them – and the sponsor's wares will be on display somewhere in the conference hall or outside it.

Choosing a venue

You could make contact with the London Tourist Board and Convention Bureau (see Useful Addresses, p. 187, for address, etc.) who have a vast number of venues all anxiously competing for business in London and the surrounding areas. The British Tourist Board can help with the rest of the United Kingdom, and almost every town in

Europe is in the business of providing venues for conferences from the United Kingdom.

You might fancy a trip to the Bahamas yourself; try and get your boss to agree to have the next conference there – there's a fairly good chance that, in your position as adviser and organizer-in-chief of the conference, to say nothing of 'just because you are his secretary', you may get your trip. It won't be much of a holiday, though, while the conference is in session or during the evenings, when you will be on duty whenever you are visible. The holiday bit might come after it is all over, before you tear back to London to write up your reports and analyses of how it all went – and count the cost!

Professional Organizers

If you are bringing delegates to the UK from abroad, professional organizers will be much the best bet, as they will be able to help with the booking of hotel accommodation and the planning of the delegates' evening activities. Many travel agents in the UK specialize in the handling of incoming groups, whether for conferences or on holiday; don't try and take that job on your own shoulders – it can be a nightmare, as everyone wants to (a) change their room, (b) change their hotel, (c) change their return flight, (d) change their theatre bookings, (e) change their wife/husband! Most of these things can be accommodated, though clearly not all, and the professional organizer can take the hell out of the whole affair (no pun intended!).

If you do decide to try and tackle the whole job yourself, which you could do if there isn't much else to your job anyway, and the conference itself is of a manageable size (you decide what's manageable!), then make sure when dealing with the venue and anyone else who is a 'supplier' that you are really communicating properly and clearly with their person in charge. Insist on finding out what is possible, on getting what you want and on getting confirmation *in writing* so that nothing is left to chance. Confirm in writing yourself on every detail – the same staff aren't always still *in situ* when your conference actually takes place as when you booked it and, anyway, they won't remember the details of *your* conference (such as what time to serve mid-morning coffee!). Make *sure* that nothing which is under *your* control can go wrong.

When you are in charge of a large, or fairly large (manageable size) conference, make sure you have regular discussion/planning meetings with everyone involved, and cover all eventualities. Insist on people doing what they said they would do at the last meeting, and sticking to the time parameters you set them. Have someone take Minutes at your planning meetings and circulate them to everyone within a day or so. Insist on people turning up to your meetings, too, and check in advance that they will be there, bringing with them whatever information is needed. Much of the initial planning consists of contacting speakers, issuing invitations to speakers and delegates, and producing a provisional programme – which usually contains suggestions for hotel accommodation (if applicable), probable costs of hotels, evening activities and the conference itself, and an initial registration form – and therefore printing of stationery is one of the early items. Probably at one of your first meetings you will decide on a conference logo, and all stationery used in connection with the conference will bear the logo from then on. Don't try and get everyone to agree on this – committee decisions on design can take a lifetime – if you have someone good on design, get them to produce a couple of designs, try and mentally approve one yourself in advance, and promote that one at the meeting. You can show the other(s) to the assembled group if you wish but, if you have a preference, make it clear. The same applies to most items where a committee decision is needed – try and 'fix' it in advance where practicable and you will save hours of valuable time.

Make a thousand, or a million, lists of *everything*. Keep a pad by your bed and, if you wake in the night with inspiration, write it on your pad and transfer it to your conference list when you get to the office. *Everything* without exception needs noting, as nothing must be left to chance. There is always the possibility of forgetting the really obvious things, as everyone assumes that someone else has thought of *that* and it gets overlooked. You even need to check the supplies of loo paper and towels at the venue – and periodically during the conference, too – since the housekeeping staff may not be as vigilant as you would like.

The banqueting staff in hotels are very helpful, but their equipment (overhead projectors, microphones, etc.) may not be state-of-the-art. Again, contact with the London Tourist Board and Convention Bureau, and a look through their annual magazine *Convention London* in particular, or their monthly one, *London Log*, can be really helpful, and all manner of services can be located in that way. The staff at the hotel/conference venue may be able to make recommendations regarding conference registration staff and recording and transcription or allied services, but are probably likely to recommend someone they know and love, rather than give an unbiased view.

After your careful preparation of the conference, you still need to keep an eye on your boss, to see that, if he is chairman of any or all of the sessions, he has his speech(es) ready and in tip-top order, and that *he knows when and where he has to be*. If, because of your organizing responsibilities, you can't keep tabs on him, make sure to delegate someone to do so, as he shouldn't be allowed to drift off to the bar two minutes before he is to chair a fringe session in a side-room (a frequent occurrence – the bar and the side-room sessions).

To summarize, there are books about conference organizing which you can and should refer to, and if there is a really big conference to organize, take professional advice and possibly employ professional conference organizers. (Try Yellow Pages if you don't know any, or see the Useful Addresses at the end of this book.)

The London Tourist Board and Convention Bureau have check-lists for conference organizers, too, so it is to be hoped that you won't miss anything out – and they can help with estimating costs and with finding the professional organizer you may eventually decide you need.

Interpreters

Interpreters come at various levels. AIIC interpreters are international, top-level conference interpreters, and are correspondingly expensive. There are people who are very good at languages, who can cope very well, but who are unused to the booth/recording-equipment situation, who can handle a small meeting, by telling a few people nearby what is going on; and there are linguists who cannot be trusted (don't ask your friend who speaks fluent French), as almost any meeting is 'technical' in one way or another.

As already mentioned under Transcripts, p. 82, interpreters' words are copyright, and if you are going to require a recording of the proceedings, their permission may well be required (they usually give it without difficulty). Conference interpreters are used to sharing a (hopefully) sound-proof booth with another interpreter of the same language, with a console connected to the sound system in front of them. They flick keys or press buttons to switch their microphones on and off, depending on the language being spoken at the time. Most qualified conference interpreters will not work for longer than about twenty minutes at a time without a break, and are qualified/bilingual in at least two languages. They probably do not recall much of what takes place in the conference hall afterwards, as they are trained to speak the words they hear straight into a microphone in another language, without inwardly digesting every word; so don't expect them to be able to remember the bits of the proceedings you can't make out on a tape.

Interpreters must be supplied, at least ten days before the conference, with as much paperwork (especially for technical meetings) as possible, i.e.

Programme

Names of speakers

Names of delegates

Papers to be presented

Diagrams, charts, etc.

so that they can check the difficult technical words in advance. The better prepared they are, the better the result will be, and the better the conference will go if the interpreters can speak smoothly through even the most difficult scientific matter.

Booths for the interpreters are frequently supplied by the recording firm, who should provide all the electronic sound equipment necessary, both to record and amplify all the languages which are used. They will supply microphones, which will be placed at an appropriate distance from the speakers so that not a word is lost, and cables will be taped to the floor where they cross it, so that there is no danger to participants, speakers or the staff at the conference hall – or you! At most international conferences, radio receivers are provided, with earphones, for the use of delegates when the language being spoken is not theirs. They tune in to the correct channel for their language, and switch off when their own language is being spoken by a speaker. The interpreters translate everything they hear and are automatically transmitted on the correct channel for the listeners.

Recording (see also page 81)

Recording firms may use a reel-to-reel machine, although it is becoming increasingly common for recordings to be made straight on to audio cassette. It is often a good idea, though, for there to be a back-up recording. Cassettes in particular are occasionally prone to poor sound-quality (due to poor recording, poor tape, or inadequate understanding by a technician), so a reel-to-reel back-up does no harm. Equally, try to have copies made of all cassettes before you part with them to be transcribed, in case they get lost, torn or destroyed, or all the recording is accidentally deleted. Copy everything before you part with it – at least you can't then be blamed if it vanishes.

Remember to check that the recording people (or you) are keeping a continuity note, otherwise it is impossible to keep track of who said what, when. To reiterate, you need:

the title of the meeting
number of tape
side A or B (or 1 or 2)
date and time of start of *each* side
name/initials of *each* speaker
and time of each speaker's contribution (including interjections from the floor, where practicable)

Translation

People asking you to arrange written translation (as opposed to interpreting) for the papers to be submitted at a meeting, and/or of the transcription of the proceedings afterwards, may not be aware that the subject-matter is 'technical'. Computer programmers having a meeting may tell you that it is not technical, but you can be sure that it is; it's just that to them it is nothing very special. Translation is a very hazardous business and should definitely be left to professionals (see the suggestions footnote on p. 126). Do *not* ask some one you know who is fluent in a language to help out; get a paid translator. That way you can complain if the job is not perfect, although with professional translation you should be handed back a perfect job. Another danger with 'amateurs' is that they may (a) not know the technical jargon, and (b) be poor translators. Translators know that it is essential to choose the right dictionaries, and they spend a good deal of time at the library mugging up on subjects that they didn't know a thing about until they received the latest piece of work to translate. Translators know that to use a dictionary is nothing to be ashamed of; on the contrary, one used well and effectively is one of the chief tools of the professional translator. Far better to use someone with an expert knowledge of the subject matter than a brilliant 'linguist' with no particular specialist knowledge of the subject. Understanding the subject will enable a translator to pick the correct and most applicable word from the dictionary.

A professional translator should be willing to have a translation sworn (witnessed by a Commissioner for Oaths and signed to this effect) signifying his/her undertaking that the translation is a true translation of the original work – this is particularly applicable when final contracts on an international deal are being signed; the translator is then responsible (and will normally carry insurance to cover any inadvertent errors) for the accuracy of the document – if he leaves off a nought in a figure in the millions of dollars or pounds, he may be held responsible for the resultant misunderstanding.

With amateur translation, although a fairly good rough approximation of the original may be produced it should not be relied upon; and where conferences, seminars, meetings, symposia, etc., are concerned, and particularly where international agreements are at stake, don't mistakenly try to economize with your company's money – it could be a costly error.

Even in less important situations, if your knowledge of the language isn't good enough to check it (not very likely, given the usual technical content of most work handed to translators), then the not-very-good translation, produced by a not-very-good translator, may end up on the desk of your boss's boss somewhere in Europe, and you, your boss and the translator will have your reputations distinctly tarnished.

Translations should be carried out only *into* the translator's mother-tongue, i.e. English translators work only *into* English from another language, and Germans translate only *into* German. However good their knowledge of a language not their own may be, they do make the odd idiomatic error, or phrase something in a way that sounds just a bit 'funny' (like those instructions that come with some Japanese radios).

In the case of an international conference, papers which are to be presented in a foreign language should be obtained many weeks before the conference starts; the translation will need checking by the author, who may understand and speak the language into which his work has been translated, even though he could not spare the time (or energy) to translate it perfectly himself. Once checked, it may have to have certain parts re-translated or at least retyped, and you don't want to leave yourself so short of time that the rough copy has to be circulated to 300 participants.

Typing of Conference Papers

The speakers' papers are often subsequently turned into a book of the conference, and all will need to be typed in a similar type-style, using a similar layout, probably designed by you; so you will have to pass on the layout instructions to the typists, taking particular care with the foreign-language typists, to ensure that their work matches, as nearly as possible, the rest.

If you have no time to prepare all the conference papers before the big day, get help with both the typing and the collating and stapling. Not the average agency 'temp', though. You need high-quality, intelligent sorting and handling and, of course, typing, particularly if the typed papers are to be presented (that is, read aloud) to the meeting by their authors.

Again, try the specialist conference transcription people (see Useful Addresses once again!). The instructions already given for the transcription of recordings of meetings (see Chapter 9, pp. 82–3) hold good here. Do not hesitate to be demanding in order to obtain the highest standards. Insist on top-quality work – in all fields of activity, of course – and you will almost certainly get it.

Pick everybody's brains on conference organizing. It is great fun, especially when you go to the conference yourself (even when no travel is involved) and can see and enjoy the fruits of your labours.

Things to remember

Invitations, registration forms

Check with venue constantly that all is well

Confirm everything to everybody in writing

Do you need direction signs at the venue?

Conference folder, with paper, pen (printed with firm's name?) programme, useful addresses, maps, instructions, information, etc.

Registration staff (you only, perhaps, for small conferences)

Photocopier, typewriter, (word processor?) within reach at venue

Recording equipment, interpreters, booths, microphones, etc.

Conference hostesses – multi-lingual?

Delegates lists – should be alphabetical

Badges (specialist firms supply the blanks) – typed in advance (best on word processor), taken from the delegates lists

Printing, printed papers

Overhead projector, flip chart

Menus . . . coffee, tea

Place names

Plus anything else which occurs to you as you use the list.

2 Office Equipment and Procedures

19 *Office Equipment*

Find out as much as you can about all the equipment you meet. Ask colleagues, get the manual, ring the manufacturer, bother the salesman. Get to know what maintenance you can and should do, and how to get repairs done.

Find out if the equipment in your office is covered by a service contract, where a flat charge is made for all the service calls necessary in a year, or whether you are charged separately for each call. There is no straightforward answer as to which is the best system. If you have a machine that functions perfectly for years, you wonder why on earth you are paying a huge sum annually for a service contract. Conversely, if you have a 'lemon' that breaks down every week, you may well be kicking yourself for not having a service contract. (Remember, too, that sometimes service contracts include spare parts when necessary, but sometimes they don't.)

In any case, before you call the repair man, check the obvious things. Is it plugged in, is it switched on, is the electricity switched on? Every repair man can tell you that he gets frequent calls from people whose cleaning staff have switched off the mains at the outlet. In the case of computer systems, they need to be connected not only to the mains but to each other – have any plugs come out? Check all the visible moving parts: have they been moved to another position? Ask colleagues – they may know the foibles of a machine, or just have had experience of some of the things that go wrong frequently.

When you do call the repair man, ask him to explain what the problem is, how and why he thinks it happened, and if he has any suggestions for avoiding difficulties in future.

Don't hesitate to ask about equipment – you won't look foolish at all. Every new model (and every old one) seems to have some feature that's different and in these days of the microchip new models seem to come out each week. You can always say, 'I've never seen one like *that* before.'

It's worth taking a look at office supplies shops, magazines, and office equipment exhibitions to see what's new. Somebody's busy inventing something to make your life easier, from the better pencil sharpener to a whole new filing system (computerized or not).

If you have to purchase new equipment, investigate not just the equipment, but the best way to pay for it – whether outright purchase, rental, hire purchase, lease hire, etc. All these arrangements have different costs, and advantages and disadvantages. Ask until you understand everything about a contract – and particularly find out whether maintenance, repairs, parts, after-sales service and training are included.

20 *Communications*

Telephones

Find out how your phones work. If you have a switchboard, you may be able to dial other extensions, or dial a number to get an outside line, or you may have to give these instructions to the switchboard operator. Visit the switchboard and meet the people who operate it (see Chapter 7, Best Friends). They will be glad to tell you all about the system, and it is friendlier to be able to address them by name when you have to ring them. In some firms the switchboard operator will dial all outside calls, in others perhaps just exchanges outside your local area – if so, be as patient and helpful as possible.

The latest switchboards have many new facilities, and the new desktop phones incorporate facilities formerly found only on switchboards (most modern switchboards in fact are only desktop size). Some of the new facilities are:

transferring a call to another extension

diverting all your calls to another extension (if you are visiting someone else's office)

diverting calls to a second extension if the first one is busy

flashing a light while the phone is in use to tell you that you have a call waiting

flashing a light to tell you that the switchboard has taken a message while you were out

remembering the number you just dialled (to ring it again if you didn't get through)

storing several frequently dialled numbers, which you can summon by one number or a short code holding the call on your line while you use the phone to ring someone else for information

conference calls: putting several extensions together so that more than two people can confer on the telephone

loudspeaker phones, so that everyone around a desk can hear the conversation

interrupting: certain people (say, the boss or supervisor) can be given the ability to interrupt the calls on other extensions

call barring: all extensions (or some of them) can be prevented from dialling long-distance calls (or permitted to dial long distance inland, but not overseas)

The switchboard itself can report on many aspects of its use. Some now have a device attached called a call-logger which keeps track of all calls (this can also be done through a microcomputer). It can produce printouts showing each number dialled, the cost and length of the call, the extension or department from which it was made, and also the number of incoming calls taken by each extension, how long it took to answer, how many calls were unanswered and so on.

The procedure for telephone instruments today is for British Telecom (BT) to install the telephone lines and sockets, into which you plug telephones which you may purchase from either BT or an independent supplier. Many of the new phones have some of the above features. You can also obtain cordless phones which let you wander a considerable distance, and telephones which connect to the new cellular network and can be used anywhere in the country, even in your car.

One thing to remember about this new telephone equipment is that many items are being sold which are not approved by BT and may therefore be incompatible or give you problems with servicing; you are not allowed to connect these to your system. Approved equipment has a clear indication on it – look for these marks where you see phones being sold. Also, before buying, check exactly what electricity supply may be needed, and what means of connection is required for your phone system: does it plug into your jack outlets (there are two types of jacks now in operation) or does it require installation and, if so, who will do it.

In addition to the usual telephone directory or directories for your area, you should have business or commercial directories (Yellow Pages) in which listings are by business rather than alphabetical. You should also have BT's dialling code booklet, containing the codes you have to dial before the number when ringing long distance in the UK or overseas (and what the time-differences are abroad). It also has information about BT services (which is also to be found in the front of telephone directories), such as directory inquiries, repairs, the weather, and even sports results and recipe of the day. Find a minute some time to leaf through both the booklet and the first few pages of the directory to familiarize yourself with the services that are available.

BT will also provide you with a pamphlet explaining their charges, and you should be aware of the approximate costs of various phone calls and the times at which they are cheapest. Don't hesitate to dial 100 to ask the operator for any information about the phone service.

Answering machines

Answering machines are widely used to answer the phone when there's no one available. They play a pre-recorded message (which you can change whenever you wish). Most people recite their telephone number, apologize that there is no one available to take the call, and ask the caller to leave his/her name and message.

The answering machine must be connected to an electricity supply and to the phone lines (either with a jack or by being actually wired in), and somebody has to remember to switch it on when you all go out, and to listen to the messages when you get back.

Answering machines can be attached to extensions, too, so that the switchboard operator doesn't have to take a message when the extension doesn't answer.

Some machines can play all your messages back to you when you ring them – that is, you ring your own number from outside, and when the call is answered you send a special sound-signal into the receiver which instructs the machine to play the message tape to you, so you can get your messages whenever you have access to a telephone.

Pagers

Many systems have been devised for locating people who are not at a telephone. Some firms have intercoms or public address systems over which you can broadcast to everyone in the area. The favourite of the moment (until the time comes when everyone has a phone in their pocket) is the radiopager, which will emit a bleeping noise to tell you to phone your office or switchboard. Some can even display a small message.

Cables

Although there is no longer a telegram service in the UK, BT operates a Telemessage service and overseas cables are still available. You can dictate the message over the telephone (and the charge appears on your phone bill). It is sent overseas (via cable or satellite) and a copy of the message is delivered to the recipient. Check first with BT about the charges, which relate to the length of the message, as you may want to compose your message in the shortest way possible.

Telex

The telex service is a worldwide link between subscribers. You must have a telex number yourself (and equipment), and you have to know the telex number of those to whom you wish to send a message. A directory of numbers is available from BT, but most subscribers put their telex number on their letterhead.

You type a message into the telex machine, the message is sent electronically, and then appears, typed out, on the recipient's machine. Charges are made according to distance and length of message sent, in addition to the annual subscription to the service. BT also has a service which will send the same message to many recipients for you. Newer telex machines permit you to type the message into the machine's memory first (and store it if you wish) and then you can correct or change it before sending (or send the same message to several people without retyping). Microcomputers, word processors and some typewriters can be used as telexes, but need additional hardware and software for such use.

Computer communications/mailboxes

There are many ways in which computers can communicate with one another, or messages can be sent using them (within your organization or to outsiders) either via telephone lines or special cables, or via mailbox services. A mailbox system means that, without a permanent link between two parties, one can send a message to an existing service, where it will be stored until the recipient asks (via computer or communications device) for his messages.

Computers can also connect you to information services, such as library catalogues, financial information services, timetables, etc. In some cases these services permit you to talk to them too, and make reservations or give orders. Some of these services are free (once you have the equipment to contact them); others require a membership fee and/or a charge when they are used.

Fax

Fax (an abbreviation of 'facsimile') machines transmit an exact copy of a document (as though it were a photocopy) from one fax machine to another. This relies on both parties having the appropriate equipment. (BT and the Post Office provide services whereby you can send a document from a fax machine locally to a fax machine in a different place – and from there the copy will be sent on to the recipient.) Fax machines are becoming more common all the time and are often used between offices where a great deal of visual material (graphs and charts, for instance) has to be exchanged.

The Post Office also operates a facsimile system called Intelpost, through a network of just over a hundred post offices around the country. They can transmit a document either to a private fax machine or to the post office nearest to the addressee. The reproduction is of photocopy standard, generally speaking, but the Post Office will accept copy for transmission only before about 4.30 in the afternoon.

21 *Dictating Machines and Calculators*

Dictating Machines

These small tape recorders usually have two units: one is to be used by the person dictating (this may have a separate microphone or one built into the recorder); this is often pocket size and portable (battery operated). The companion play-back or transcription unit is usually non-portable, it has an attached earphone or headpiece (to help reduce distracting background sounds) and foot pedal (to start and stop the tape without taking the hands off the keyboard), as well as controls for speed, volume and tone, and a counter to locate a particular place on the tape.

In some instances, the same machine is used for both dictating and transcribing and has to be passed back and forth between boss and secretary. Sometimes the boss uses a desktop machine for dictating in the office, but carries a miniature recorder to dictate and make notes away from his desk. Remember that, in addition to dictating letters, your boss may want to give you messages in this form.

Many systems have a means of noting information about the dictation on a card on the machine, such as at what point on the tape a letter starts and ends, or where a message or an urgent letter will be found. Some people at first need a few hints on how to make machine dictation easier for you; for example, you need to know whether to expect a long or short letter.

The cassette tapes used come in three or more sizes: micro and mini (which look almost the same but are not interchangeable) and the larger standard audio cassette (the kind you use in your cassette recorder at home). Adaptors are available to allow transcription from any of these sizes on special playback sets but, generally speaking, you will have to get the right cassette for your system (so take one with you when you go shopping).

Normally a cassette tape is simply used again after the dictation has been transcribed. The sounds on it are automatically erased when you record on it again. Occasionally you may want to keep a tape and not re-use it. Label it (clearly: not just 'lr of 11.12', but 'dealers' contract dictated by Mr B, 11 December 1996'), put it away somewhere safe. For absolute security, there is a way to prevent re-recording: read the instructions that come with your cassettes. Usually this is done by breaking off a small piece of plastic (and can be 'undone' by using a bit of sticky tape to cover that area of the cassette).

You must have a system that will allow you to keep track of (i) tapes awaiting transcription, (ii) tapes that have been partially transcribed but are not finished, and (iii) tapes that are finished and ready for re-use. (Try to avoid having a 'miscellaneous' category – you don't know what's on them, when it was dictated, whether it was transcribed, etc.) You might decide to have a supply of labels for the cassettes themselves, or to number the cassettes and note each use in a register. Make sure that, when your boss comes looking for a tape in your absence, he can find a usable one (and that he can't lay his hands on one that you haven't yet transcribed, thus losing for ever his earlier dictation by re-recording over the top of it).

Calculators

These small arithmetic machines have a great variety of extra functions available, in addition to doing simple maths. They may have a memory or memories in which to store a figure you want to use repeatedly in calculations, or even a formula; they may do percentages, or they may automatically do conversions, say from metric to imperial measures. Not all facilities are available on every calculator, and sometimes the procedures for use differ slightly – as always, read the instructions.

Calculators come in many different sizes, too, from the so-called 'credit card' pocket size to quite substantial desktop models, some with rolls of paper for printing out the figures.

When purchasing one, make sure it has the facilities you need – you must ask, or read the instructions thoroughly beforehand. And if you ask, it's a good idea to have the machine demonstrated to you before you buy. Satisfy yourself that it is comfortable to use and that you can read the display clearly. Make sure it can display enough digits for the numbers you are likely to use – many small calculators have only eight-digit displays, which only takes you up to £999 999.99 and is consequently useless for millionaires.

If you use a calculator a lot, it's worth having one which can be run directly off mains electricity (or can be adapted to do so), rather than running out of batteries frequently. Or try the new solar-cell ones, which get enough energy from natural or artificial light, and never need batteries. If you do get a battery-operated calculator, it's best to have one that turns itself off after a few minutes if you forget to do it.

22 *Typewriters*

Most typewriters in offices today are electric. You get to a new line by use of the carriage return key – usually at the right of the keyboard. The electric typewriter also ensures that each key hits the paper with the same force, giving an even impression with no effort on your part. Some electric typewriters, instead of having keys which strike the paper and a carriage which moves the paper along, have a small spherical 'element' containing all the characters, known as a golf-ball, and this moves across the paper and revolves to strike the required character against the ribbon and thus print on the paper.

Even newer are the electronic typewriters. Many of the mechanical working parts of the older machines have been replaced by the microchip, and the printing is done by a circular print element called a daisywheel (each petal of the 'daisy' carries a character, and the element turns to position the appropriate letter as a key is struck).

Daisywheels and golfballs can be removed and replaced in order to change to one with a different typeface (such as italics or one with scientific symbols) or in order to use a different type size (10, 12 or 15 characters to the inch – this is known as 'pitch'). If you have changed the size, in addition to changing the element, you will have to set a lever on the typewriter to the appropriate pitch. There is a small lever atop a golfball which releases it for replacement or cleaning. Daisywheels have various mechanisms for removing and changing them; do remember they are fragile and must be handled carefully to prevent distortion. Nowadays they sometimes come in a plastic drop-in cartridge.

Your typewriter manual will give instructions for replacing print elements, changing ribbons or ribbon cartridges, correction tapes, etc.

Many electric and electronic typewriters have a correction key. This is a special key (usually at the lower right of the keyboard) which both backspaces and activates a 'lift-off' tape; this is a separate small spool of tape which, when pressed against the paper, actually lifts off the printed character. It must be used in combination with the appropriate 'correctable' typewriter ribbon. On some typewriters you must strike the mistake again to remove it, then press the correct key; on others, however, the typewriter will remember which key you struck in error, and it will automatically both backspace and remove the error.

Memory typewriters

Electronic typewriters can now contain a 'memory'. Some remember just a few characters (enough to correct a mistake, as above), some a line, some a few lines, or as much as a page or a few pages. Some even have add-on memory units for permanent storage on disks.

There is often a one- or two-line display (liquid crystal, like the display on a calculator or watch) on the front so that you can see what is in the memory or type in a line and correct it before it prints; and some have a small screen. These typewriters are well on the way to becoming word processors; each new model seems to have another facility (for example, a spelling check which beeps at you if you type a word it does not recognize).

Another very useful facility on some memory typewriters (or word processors) is the provision of a decimal tab stop. This permits you to tab to a column of figures and then type the figure without calculating whether its decimal point will be exactly under the one above. If you have figures of different sizes – say £5.16, £10.25, £308.49 – and you just tab to the column and start typing, they will look like this:

£5.16

£10.25

£308.49

With a decimal tab they will look like this:

  £5.16

 £10.25

£308.49

If they are whole numbers, without a decimal point, the list will still be arranged with the last digit of each number underneath the one before.

Some memory typewriters will store phrases that you use frequently; and if they have even a one-page memory, they will store a letter for you to send to several different people without the necessity of retyping it each time.

All typewriters should be kept clean, both outside and inside, and protected by a cover from dust and spillages. You can clean the outside with a damp cloth or special cleaners. You can gently clean the inside with a soft brush, unless your manual or dealer tells you not to. (Generally speaking, the older the model the more amateur cleaning it can take.) Keys can be cleaned with a stiff brush, and there are cleaning kits for print elements. Don't drop things in typewriters – many service calls are required just to fish out a paperclip or drawing pin – either of which can make a typewriter malfunction without it being obvious what is wrong.

23 *Word Processors*

Word processors (or microcomputers functioning as word processors) permit you to type your text into the machine's memory, and then correct or change it before printing it out. The text can also be stored (usually on floppy disks) so that you can re-use it or change it at a later date.

A word processor is really a one-purpose microcomputer, dedicated only to word processing, and hence sometimes called a 'dedicated word processor'.

In some offices a word processor totally replaces the typewriter, and is used for all typing. Sometimes a limited number are available for special tasks, such as:

> sending form letters: instead of having to retype these each time, you summon up a copy of the letter and only have to type in the new name and address
>
> sending the same letter to a number of people: both the letter and the lists of names and addresses can be kept on file, and the word processor can automatically produce a separate letter to each person. This is called a 'mail merge' function. In some cases the letter can be automatically varied for each recipient, inserting the correct information at a particular point, or adding a 'customized' line or paragraph where needed
>
> storing copies of lengthy documents (leases, contracts, architects' specifications, etc.) so that, when you need such a document, only the new information and any revisions have to be retyped – not the whole thing.

Some of the facilities you would expect on a word processor are:

> you can correct text on the screen before it is printed out

you can store this text on a disk

you can ask to see it again to re-use it or change it

you can move a section of the text to any location in the document

you can search through the text automatically for any word or phrase

you can change a word automatically throughout the text

you may have an automatic dictionary that will check your spelling (but it won't catch mis-usages, or 'there' for 'their' or 'its' for 'it's') and you will be able to add new words to it – perhaps specialist words used in your business or difficult names you often use.

Each dedicated word processor (and the various forms of word processing software available for microcomputers) works in a different way, using different keys or commands to perform its functions – which is a nuisance because each new system you meet you have to re-learn. But once you have learnt one system, you will be familiar with the concepts, and will need less training in future.

There are courses available to learn a particular system, or sometimes several systems at a time (if you want to temp), and when you buy a word processor training is usually given.

What does it look like?

The first thing you will notice about a word processor is that you have a screen – or monitor, or visual display unit (VDU) – on which you will see displayed whatever you have typed in or have called up from the memory, and the instructions you give. The display on the screen can be in a number of entertaining colours, usually on a black background. Favourites are green, orange, and plain old white. Much research has been done to find out which colour combinations are most comfortable, but as yet there has been no clear-cut answer. On full-colour monitors you can change the colour of the text as well as the colour of the background, and this is fun; but it is a facility not often available on ordinary word processor screens.

What you can usually control is the degree of brightness (by a control knob somewhere on the monitor). You can also move the monitor physically to avoid reflections on the screen; some others are on a movable pedestal. If the information on the screen is flickering or moving about, complain and get it fixed, as this is very tiring. Many people feel that the amount of time you spend looking at a monitor should be limited, or that you should have frequent breaks.

Your keyboard is laid out in the same way as your typewriter keyboard, but probably with a lot of extra keys around it. The extra keys are shortcuts to giving necessary commands and you will learn about them as you learn to use the system.

The disk drive unit (which also contains the microchips that do the work) is usually positioned under the monitor. Some are attached, some are in a separate box and can be moved to the side if you want. Sometimes the disk drive(s) are positioned under or to the side of your desk. There will be a slot, or slots, into which floppy disks are placed to operate the machine. There will also be a printer, somewhat resembling a typewriter, where the work is printed out.

All of this machinery is known in computer terms as 'hardware', because it is hard and you can touch it. The instructions or 'programs' given to a computer to make it function are known as 'software' – it is intangible and you cannot see it.

In some instances you will have only one part of a computer system on your desk – just the monitor and keyboard. The processing unit, the memory unit and even the printer can be located in another place – possibly being shared by several of these 'terminals', of which yours is one.

If you store personal data about people on your computer, your firm may have to be registered under the Data Protection Act (1984), which sets up regulations to prevent unauthorized use or disclosure of information.

24 Printers

Microcomputers and word processors (and telex machines) have printers which can sometimes double as electric typewriters. Printers are most often one of two main types. One uses the daisywheel elements also found on electronic typewriters – but, because these print much faster than you can type, they do make an awful clatter. The other common type is the dot-matrix printer. The print element on these is a bundle of pins. The correct combination of pins sticks out to form the shape of the letter required, and then retracts and reforms for the next one. The pins press against a ribbon to create the image on the paper, so you can see if you look closely that the image is made up of single dots from each pinhead. If the dots are very close together, they appear to be a solid line and thus of 'letter quality'. Dot-matrix printers are generally faster and a bit cheaper than daisywheel printers, though the print quality is never quite as good. They make a horrible noise, too.

Covers and hoods are available to minimize the noise from any type of printer, and some offices are planned so that the printer is behind a partition or screen. Manufacturers are well aware of this problem and are constantly developing quieter printers, so noise is a factor to consider if you are buying one.

There are also thermal printers; these require special paper to form the image, and this technology also appears on a few typewriters. Thermal printers are very quiet. Ink-jet printers squirt a jet of ink at the paper; they are most often used where it is necessary to print several colours on a page, as they contain ink in the primary colours and mix these to make other shades.

Laser printers silently and swiftly create a page of text in a fashion similar to the way it is done on photocopiers, but as yet they are rather more expensive than other types of printer.

If you are using a printer for a small quantity of letters, you may be able to insert each piece of paper (or sandwich of paper and carbon paper) in the same way as you do on a typewriter. Sheet feeders are available which hold a quantity of paper and drop another sheet into the printer when necessary. These are usually used when preparing form letters on daisywheel printers.

But if you want a printer (usually a dot-matrix) to do large quantities of work quickly and unattended, you need a 'tractor feed' which will use 'continuous stationery' of the sort that has holes on the sides and is pulled through the printer without attention. This paper comes in one long piece with perforations at each page-end where it is folded, so that it can be torn along them into single sheets.

After a job is done on this type of paper, the decision has to be made whether to remove the strip containing the holes on each side of the paper. Some people like to remove the strip on documents that are going out of the office, because they look neater. Some people remove it in order to leave the paper the proper size to fit into files or binders. And yet others leave it on, either to save themselves the trouble or to make use of the holes to fasten the paper into special binders.

There are machines that 'burst' this type of paper into separate sheets, and strip the edges, if it is necessary to do the job quickly and in large quantities.

25 *Disks/Discs*

People use both spellings of the word; some call them diskettes, and some abbreviate floppy disks to just 'floppies'. In any case, the disk is an important part of your computer or word processor system. It is the equivalent of recording tape (which is also used on some computers) and is used for permanent storage of programs (software) and the information you type into your computer.

In addition to floppy disks, there are also hard disks with much greater storage capacities; however, as they are permanently installed in your disk drive unit, you won't see one or have to touch it.

Floppy disks are a bit like LPs for your hi-fi, but smaller and softer. And unlike music records, disks can be recorded on, erased, and re-recorded. Computer disks now come in four sizes: 8-inch, 5¼-inch, 3½-inch and 3-inch.

In addition to knowing what size of disk your computer or word processor uses, you must be aware that they come in different types as well. There are single-sided single-density disks, single-sided double-density disks, double-sided single-density disks, and double-sided double-density disks and so forth. Before you have to order them or shop for them, find out which you need.

The 8-inch and 5¼-inch disks are permanently encased in a flexible folder so that you can handle them safely, provided you do it carefully. The 3½- and 3-inch disks are permanently enclosed in a hard cover and therefore are a little less fragile.

Each disk will have a sleeve or case to keep it in. Replace it immediately when you take it out of the computer.

To avoid writing on the label on the disk itself, you can number both disk and cover, and then list (and re-list when necessary) the complete contents of the disk on its cover.

It is good practice to keep a register of all disks and their contents in a book kept for this purpose. Use a page for each numbered disk and list all the material that has been recorded on that disk. It is really worth while spending whatever time and trouble may be necessary to make sure that finding out which disk contains what information is easy. If you have to hunt for a document you want to revise, you can easily waste as much time in the search as it would have taken you to retype it.

It is easy to damage a disk by careless handling. They won't survive being bent (and so require special protection if you have to send them by post). They must not be stored in too warm a place (not on the radiator, the window-ledge, or on the back shelf of a car). They shouldn't be left scattered on your desk where anything can be rested on them accidentally, or left where anything can be spilled on them. They may look like a suitable mat to put a coffee mug on, but they are not.

Do not write on the disk with anything hard, such as a ballpoint pen or pencil. Write the label before fixing it on to the disk. Keep a supply of *soft* felt-tip pens if you have to write on a label that is already on a disk.

Never touch the surface of the disk itself; there is a little bit visible in a slot in its permanent protective cover – this is not the place to hold it by. It is a place where a fingerprint can be fatal. A fingerprint or a bit of dust is like a mountain to the disk drive that has to 'play' these records.

You may have heard recording tape or disks referred to as 'magnetic media'. As on audio and video tapes, electromagnetism is the means for storing information on disks – and for erasing it. Therefore magnets can scramble or erase the data on disks. Look around to see if you have any – they are great for keeping paperclips together or hanging up the scissors and letter opener, but keep magnets away from disks or recording tape (cassettes, too). Often screwdrivers are magnetized, as are clips or tools that have been kept on a magnet, and there is magnetism in hi-fi speakers and telephones.

The disk drive(s) of a word processor or computer (where you put the disks in) need attention, too, in order to keep your disks in good condition. Their doors should be kept closed when not in use, to prevent dust getting in. The drives should be cleaned occasionally with a cleaning disk or one of the many kits available which use a special fluid on a cleaning disk. Take the advice of your supplier or dealer, or check shops and catalogues for details of the many cleaning kits available.

Many types of storage box are available for disks, though you yourself may have clever ideas about how to adapt a box or desk drawer for this purpose. Keep the storage area clean – there's not much sense putting disks away in a box that has accumulated dust and crumbs. And you should have a second storage area available for the 'back-up' copies of your disks, so that all your eggs are not in one basket. Most boxes have a lock to prevent unauthorized access. If yours is supposed to be locked, lock it. And do something sensible with the key. (But make sure at least one other person knows where it is.)

The information stored on disks is often very valuable and not easily replaceable. It is essential to have made 'back-up' copies of all disks so that, if the original is damaged in some way, you have a copy. You should have a procedure to ensure that copies are not kept in the same place as the originals: sometimes a member of staff takes home the back-up copies, sometimes they are put in a safe for protection both against people and against fire and flood. Don't ever be careless about these procedures. Think about what would happen if a disk or disks were lost or destroyed. The result could be total disaster for your company – or it could mean hours of retyping for you.

26 *Photocopiers*

It is usual today for most offices to have some copying facilities available. It may be a desktop copier, or you may have to go to the printroom or copying room of a large organization. If you're in a small office without a copier, you may have to go out to the nearest shop that has one.

The very latest copiers have not just one standard size of reduction or enlargement, but are equipped with a zoom lens that can make a copy in a variety of sizes. They can also copy just part of an original if you prefer, and make it the right size to fit in with another original. This is called a cut-and-paste facility, and removes the need actually to cut up and paste together several pieces of paper to make up a page. Alternatively, if you want just one column of a newpaper article, or one paragraph of an original, you don't have to cut it out or block off the rest of the page.

There are also full-colour copiers that can make colour copies of coloured originals. These are expensive and only a few firms have them; but if you need colour copies, there is usually a copy bureau nearby that can do them.

Some copiers can use a coloured toner (instead of black) to make the print on the page a different colour from black. This is done by having trays containing the coloured toner. In some models you can use just one colour at a time, by removing and replacing the tray; others can hold more than one colour at a time.

Maintenance

If you have to keep the photocopier running, you will be shown how to do it. Even if it's not your responsibility, it's good to learn about it – they always seem to need attention at awkward times. The machine will have a manual or instruction book – if not, the manufacturer can supply you with one.

Most photocopiers use ordinary paper and hold a supply of it in easily removable trays. If the copier doesn't work, this is the first thing to check. Make sure the paper fits the tray properly and isn't creased, as this will cause a paper jam.

Paper jams occur when the paper gets caught or crumpled in the mechanism in some way. It is then necessary to open the copier to try to find out where it is caught, and remove it. Some machines can open in more than one place when you are looking for the jammed paper. Do this carefully, as the insides are often very hot. Instructions will be in the manual, or printed on the machine (or on the inside of the door you open). In many instances you have to press a 'reset' button to restore the machine to operation.

Some machines require liquids that have to be replaced when they run out; some need cylinders of powder (toner); and some have waste toner that has to be removed in some way. These jobs are usually very easy and not really messy nowadays. Most copiers indicate their needs by flashing a message or a symbol on their 'control panel'. Make sure that you have plentiful supplies of whatever the machine may want. There is a law that says the machine will suddenly demand attention when you already have a panic on, anyway!

Don't forget that you can use coloured paper in the copier. It's often useful to colour-code memos or regularly produced documents (you won't confuse the blue one with last month's report, which was pink).

You can also copy on to transparent plastic sheets that can be used in overhead projectors. These machines project on to a screen (like a movie screen) the image of whatever you put into their base, and are often used for showing material to a meeting, rather than having to pass round one original or copies.

There are also the pages of labels that can be photocopied, and now there are pages of transparent adhesive material that you can put through the photocopier.

27 *Stencils*

Although it is rather an out-dated method, you may find that for making very large numbers (hundreds) of copies of a document, your office uses the more economical duplicating machine, and it is worth while being prepared to know how to work one. In order to use these machines, the original must be prepared on a special waxy paper called a stencil.

Typing on a stencil is also known as 'cutting a stencil' because the impression of the keys actually cuts into the waxy surface. You can also draw on a stencil or mark out lines with a special tool.

In order to get the right impression on the stencil, you want the keys of your typewriter (or golfball or daisywheel) to hit the stencil directly, rather than through the typewriter ribbon. All typewriters have a switch to allow this to happen. You should find out where this control is anyway, because, if it is inadvertently moved, you will fail to get any impression on your paper when you type and will wonder what is wrong. So it's one of the things you check before calling the repair man. Find it and try it out.

On some typewriters there is a ribbon control switch on the front of the typewriter that is colour coded. When it is set to black, the ribbon is being used; when it is set to white, you are ready to type on a stencil. In some cases there is also a red setting, which means the bottom (or red) half of a two-colour ribbon is being used. Sometimes the control is on the mechanism that holds the ribbon cassette and you have to open the top of the typewriter to gain access to it.

If you make a mistake while typing on a stencil, you must cover the mistake with a special fluid to seal up the waxy surface again so that you have a smooth surface to type the correction on. Sometimes this fluid is red (which makes all your corrections very noticeable on the stencil – but they won't show up on the copies), but a white or neutral colour is often available nowadays.

You will need to be shown how to mount the stencil on the machine, and be provided with the paper supply and the ink that will be used. If the printroom or some other person normally runs the copies for you, see if they will show you how to work it. It's fun . . . and you will have learnt another skill.

28 *Filing Systems*

What's the simplest filing system you can imagine? Perhaps one or two file folders labelled 'bills', 'letters' and so on. Or an accordion file which has a section for each letter of the alphabet and expands and contracts like an accordion.

More often, we tend to use filing cabinets of two, three or four drawers each. They can usually hold files of foolscap size – many people use these even when most of their papers are A4 size (but some are big enough only for A4). There are also shelves, known as vertical files, which hold file folders upright. Many file drawers have rods along the sides to hold the supports of filing folders so that they don't slump in the drawer. These are known as suspension files. Some people put an interior folder in these hanging files, which then don't have to be removed from the drawer.

There are various ways of indicating that, although a file exists, it has been temporarily removed. Ideally, the special card or indicator that is put in when a file is removed should tell you who has it or where it is, so that it can be retrieved if you need it urgently.

Some people put papers loose into files; others like them fastened together (or to the file folder) in a certain way, and there are many fastening systems. It takes a little longer to put a piece of paper away when it needs to be fastened in; but they don't get lost (on the other hand, you can lose the entire file instead of just one letter), they don't get out of order (you should check when putting a paper away to keep it in order by date – obviously the most recent on top), and the system discourages people from borrowing an item from the file.

There are also card-index files – boxes containing cards and separators to sort them into categories – and many types of visible displays for information that can be kept on cards.

If old files are rarely referred to but must still be kept, you can get cardboard boxes or files to keep them in which are much cheaper than everyday filing cabinets, though not quite as convenient to use.

It's a good idea to look through an office supply shop or catalogue to get an idea of the various equipment and systems available.

People have invented automatic filing systems in which files are stored in such a way that only the one you have asked for becomes accessible. This saves space, but is expensive and relies on good organization – you can't 'browse' through the filing cabinet, hoping to recognize something.

Filing systems can also be computerized: documents are scanned electronically, the information stored in a computer, and you can then look at it on screen or print it out when required. This is also likely to be known by a fancier name than 'filing system', and be called 'document storage and retrieval'.

29 *Microfilm/Microfiche*

In order to reduce the space needed for keeping large quantities of files, some companies use microfilm or microfiche. In some instances it is used only for making duplicate copies of very important papers, and then the film is kept in a safe or strongroom.

Microfilm is simply a photograph of documents, very much reduced in size, usually on reels of movie film. Microfiche is a small index-card-size piece of film which contains tiny photos of several pages of text on each piece. You may have seen microfiche in a library, as this is often the way their indexes are kept.

In either case, you need a special viewer (or projector) to be able to read the documents that are stored in this way. It needs a light source and a magnifier so that you can see the information. Some 'readers' can also print out a copy of the document you want to look at.

Commercial services exist that will photograph your files and make the film or fiches for you, if you haven't enough material to warrant investing in the equipment yourself.

All film should be handled carefully and replaced in its storage container immediately after use. The films are sometimes kept in cassettes to avoid unnecessary handling, and the fiches can be slipped into sleeves or pockets in the pages of a book.

As with any filing system, efficiency relies on your being able to find what you want when you want it. It must be well organized, there should be a way to indicate who has temporarily removed a film or fiche, and the film or fiche must be put back in the right place – it's easy to misfile a small fiche . . . and very hard to find it again.

30 Supplies

Paper

Most offices now use paper of A4 size. This 'A' series of paper sizes means that A5 is half the size of A4, while A3 is twice the size of A4, and so on:

A3 297 mm × 420 mm (11¾" × 16½")
A4 210 mm × 297 mm (8¼" × 11¾")
A5 148 mm × 210 mm (5⅞" × 8¼")

Some people still use British Standard sizes, the most common of which are quarto (8" × 10") and foolscap (8" × 13"). Paper is normally sold in reams (500 sheets), though smaller packets may be available in some stationers (a quire = 24 sheets).

Paper comes in different weights or thicknesses. Flimsy or 'bank' paper is usually used for carbon copies, bond paper for letterhead and top copies. Bond paper comes in weights of so many grammes per square metre – medium-weight paper is about 80 g/m^2.

Paper is not cheap these days, and we are all aware that saving paper saves trees. So don't just throw it all in the bin. Many people save scrap paper that can be re-used for drafts or notes: the letter you had to discard, or the extra photocopies that didn't get used. It's also becoming common practice to re-use envelopes – particularly the large or the padded ones. You can stick a label over the previous address, or buy special labels from conservation organizations.

It is also possible to buy various sorts of recycled paper, both for computer printout and for ordinary correspondence. And conversely, if you do throw out large quantities of paper, try to see if it can go to a conservation organization, so that it can be processed and re-used.

Computer printers need 'continuous' paper rather than single sheets. This paper comes in various sizes and is perforated and folded at the bottom of each sheet. At each side edge it has a strip with perforated holes to hook on to the sprockets in the printer. As they turn, the paper is pulled up through the printer. You can obtain this paper in sets with carbon paper, and it can be printed with your letterhead, or with forms such as invoices.

Envelopes

You may be able to save some time by using self-sealing envelopes that do not have to be moistened. Some people favour window envelopes, whereby you must fold the letter so that the name and address appear in the window in the envelope, and you don't have to type the address on the envelope separately. Others think that everything that arrives in a window envelope looks like a bill and may get treated in the same way, and prefer to see a typed address on the envelope. Letterheadings designed to be used with window envelopes have a line or dot to indicate where the name and address should be typed. In any case, you should check when the letter is put in the envelope, to make sure that the address is actually visible through the window.

Labels

Labels can be obtained in many, many sizes and shapes. Those used for addresses usually come in a long roll which can be put in the typewriter (like continuous stationery) or on sheets with two or three columns of eight labels each to a page. Be a little careful with labels in the typewriter or printer, as they have a tendency to peel off and get stuck on the roller.

Don't forget the sheets of labels that you can use in your photocopier, mentioned in Chapter 33, Outgoing Post.

Carbon paper

Almost everyone makes one or two carbon copies of each letter typed. You can also obtain very thin carbon paper if you need to make many copies at the same time (so that the bulk of paper in the typewriter is not too thick). Keep an eye on the bottom carbon copies, and when they are getting even a little faint, throw that piece of carbon paper away. Most carbon paper today is not paper but thin plastic. It should be kept flat so that it does not get folds or wrinkles, and it is good practice to keep your unused supplies in their original box or wrapper, as they deteriorate with age and exposure to air. Don't order too much carbon paper at one time.

Check out 'carbonless paper', which produces an image on the second and further copies by pressure alone (and a chemical coating on the paper). Some sets of forms come with disposable carbon paper which is used only once and then thrown away.

Ribbons

It is astonishing how many different sizes and shapes of ribbons are available for typewriters and printers, and equally astonishing how few are interchangeable; so you must go shopping with the old ribbon, or a note of the make and model of the machine, when you need a new one.

In older machines, ribbons come on spools and you have to rewind the old one on to one spool which is then thrown away and replaced with a new one. This messy job is unnecessary on newer machines which use so-called ribbon cassettes. The old cassette is released by a lever, the new one is inserted and the lever replaced, without much need to touch the ribbon itself. Just as sizes and shapes of cassettes differ, so do the procedures for replacement. Sometimes there is a diagram on the outside of the box; in any case, the instructions are always in the manual for the machine itself.

The ribbon itself is one of two main sorts. Ribbons made from fabric (cotton, rayon, nylon or silk) can be used over and over again until they get very faint. Carbon ribbons (which are like a long tape of plastic-based carbon paper) are used once and then thrown away.

Because you always type on a new piece of the ribbon, the blackness of the impression is exactly the same each time and very crisp and clear. (And it needn't be blackness – you can get ribbons in other colours, too.) There is no way of rewinding and re-using a carbon ribbon – so when it runs out (at 4.30 on Friday afternoon with six letters yet to be typed?) make sure you have another available.

Correction ribbons or tapes

If your typewriter has a correction ribbon, again there are two sorts. One puts white on top of your error to make it invisible. The other actually lifts off the impression of the ribbon and leaves the paper clean. These latter are called, understandably, 'lift off' tapes, and must be used in combination with a 'correctable' typewriter ribbon.

As in the case of the ribbon itself, you must get the right correction tape for your make and model of machine.

31 *Housekeeping*

You live here at work seven hours a day, often longer than you spend awake at home. Your office should be efficient, smart and comfortable. It may well be possible for you to have some influence on your environment and surround yourself with whatever you find beautiful or useful, bearing in mind that it is a shared environment and one person's poster may be another's blot on the wall.

You should consider yourself responsible for the environment, whether you have to arrange for cleaning or even take a duster to the desktop yourself. Office cleaners are often understandably reluctant to apply sprays and elbow grease to complicated equipment, so perhaps a cleaning kit is available for you to use on your high-tech machinery or, in the case of computers, specialist cleaning staff can be called in.

If you have facilities for making coffee and tea, or even for preparing lunches, work out a sensible arrangement so that no one feels hard done by and claims to be constantly doing the washing up. There are many types of coffee and hot drinks machines available for purchase or hire. If you're stuck with a really awful one, do some research and then suggest an alternative to your boss. Also, it ought to be possible to have a drink of water without having to stoop to a tap over the handbasin in the lavatory.

Fresh air is important and should be provided, even in the sealed, air-conditioned office building. An exhaust fan is often a useful means for changing the air and getting rid of smoke or the smell of lunch. There are also desktop air purifiers to minimize annoyance to non-smokers.

Equipment can and should have covers to protect it from dust and dirt. Even if it's an odd size, there are firms that make custom covers – and will even add your firm's logo if you wish. And when you have them, use them. Where is your typewriter cover? It probably came with one. Oh yes, scrunched up in the bottom of the supply cupboard. But it can make a difference.

Office chairs can usually be adjusted for different heights and degrees of back support. Desk lamps should be available and movable for comfort. Many computer screens (VDUs) can be adjusted for height and angle – if not, a turntable or base can be provided. Instead of having to keep your head bowed down to copy from a paper or your shorthand notebook, you can use a copystand and keep your chin up. A stand on an anglepoise fitting can be adjusted to any height or angle.

Speak up immediately if something is uncomfortable or you think it may be dangerous. One of the problems of today's office, which has acquired quantities of electrical equipment without having been planned for it, is the proliferation of cables and flexes running from the power points across the floor, behind the desk and around each other. There are special gadgets to fasten cables to walls and desks, or to hold them firmly on the floor. Don't risk tripping yourself, or someone else, or pulling a machine off the desk.

Floor and door mats are used for several reasons: to catch the dirt before it gets into the office; to minimize damage to floor coverings in areas of heavy usage, such as under a chair; or to reduce the static electricity that can sometimes create problems with machinery or even give nasty shocks.

Find out who is responsible for minor repairs and how to ask for them. You may have to get outside help for some things, and if you are in charge of the office it's a good idea to have a list of people you can call on – electricians, plumbers, etc. Make a point of seeing your office cleaner occasionally: to find out what he is responsible for, sometimes to remind him of what needs to be done . . . and how about a 'thank you' once in a while.

32 *Safety*

Electricity

People always used to be advised to turn all electrical equipment off at the mains at the end of the day. Now you have to think carefully about what should be turned off when not in use and what should be left on, and whether the mains should be switched off at all.

A lot of equipment has a little light to tell you that it is connected to an electrical supply, but since both red and green lights are used, colour is no help. If it's glowing there's electricity somewhere. The light may mean 'in use' or only 'ready for use'.

Some word processors and memory typewriters will lose their memory when the electricity is turned off at the mains, although not when their on–off switch is turned off. If you have one of these machines, it is wise to put a piece of sticky tape over the mains switch and a clear notice near it.

Before you leave the office, stop and think about what should be turned off, both for economy and for safety. (And, of course, what should be switched on, such as the answering machine.)

As was said in Chapter 30, Housekeeping, make sure that electrical flexes are safe and won't trip anyone up.

Fire

Every office should have a notice posted about what to do in case of fire. You should know how to notify the fire brigade, or whom to notify, how to get out of the building, where to go, and what you are responsible for under the circumstances. Take fire drills seriously – they can save lives. And also take seriously the requirements of the fire inspectors with regard to which doors must be kept shut or must not be locked shut. This is sometimes inconvenient and sometimes difficult to reconcile with security arrangements, but being able to get out in case of fire is the first priority.

First Aid

There should be a first-aid box, together with instructions about what to do in case of accident, and these should be easily and readily available at all times. No, a box of sticking plasters in a drawer somewhere is not enough. You can take a first-aid course – or someone should!

There are regulations pertinent to your office environment in the Health and Safety at Work Act (1974) and in the Offices, Shops and Railway Premises Act (1963), which set forth various responsibilities of employers. Employees are also required to take responsibility for their own health and safety and that of their co-workers. These Acts are available from Her Majesty's Stationery Office; you can also get advice from your local authority.

33 *Security*

These are evil times, they say (but haven't they always said that?), and we must be aware of security measures in our offices as well as in our homes.

You and your possessions

If you work for a large organization they may have security guards – find out how to call them *before* you need help. There may be identification cards for each employee and procedures for checking on who is admitted to the premises.

Some people now work in open-plan shared office space, and this obviously requires more care, as you won't be in a position to recognize every person you meet. If you are in a small firm, in its own premises, you may have more control over security measures. Take them seriously, in any case.

If filing cabinets or cupboards are kept locked, work out a system so that you always remember to lock them. Then work out a secure place to keep the keys. Some people use a lockable cupboard in which they keep all the office keys . . . but where is the key to this cupboard kept? On a hook beside it?

In large buildings which are open to the public, alarms are sometimes installed so that you can call for help if you need it. The women's lavatory can be provided with an alarm button, and with mirrors so that you can see if anyone is loitering there.

The most obvious things in need of protection are the petty cash, the stamps, and any small items of equipment that could easily be picked up and stowed away, such as calculators, recorders, etc. But most intruders are just after your purse. If you can't guard the door and meet everyone who comes in, make sure that your possessions are in a sensible place. Perhaps you can lock your purse in a drawer when you leave your desk – if not, take it with you – and remember not to leave coats or jackets hanging up in public with a wallet in the pocket.

Your employer's possessions and information

It is astonishing how many things go missing from offices. There are two main ways of avoiding this. One is physical: typewriters and computers can be fastened to desks. The other is the exercise of vigilance and common sense. Don't let strangers walk around unchallenged. You can ask if they are looking for someone, whether they need help – and do it so politely that the important visitor is pleased at being met so efficiently, while the thief realizes that he won't get away with something unobserved. If a repair man calls to take away a piece of equipment, check his written authorization to do so and confirm this with whoever ordered the repair. Don't be at all embarrassed to ask politely about what is going on.

Don't forget to close and fasten the windows when you go out, and clearly establish who is responsible for locking up. If you have a safe, make sure it is never left open, and be sure also that no one can watch while it is being opened.

It is useful to have a complete list of equipment, including make, model and serial number, so that it can be traced in case of theft. Pens are also available which can put your name on equipment in an ink that will be visible only under ultra-violet light; or a name can be engraved or incised on equipment. Your local police can advise you on this and on all matters of security.

Information about your employer's business is also valuable and must be protected. There are three main ways that information gets into the hands of people who shouldn't have it: first, by leaving papers visible or available; secondly, by letting unauthorized people get access to information on computers; and thirdly, by word of mouth. Don't leave an entertaining collection of information on your desk or your boss's desk for callers to read while waiting. This applies to visitors from within your organization as well as outsiders. If they should know, they will be told (rather than getting a glimpse of, say, the memo detailing someone's dismissal or salary change).

Papers thrown away can also provide information. Some firms use paper shredders to destroy this source, and some even have incinerators to destroy waste paper thoroughly.

Computers are sometimes kept physically locked, or access to information is controlled by passwords. If there is a lock, the key should be in a sensible place. If that place is the pocket of the person using the computer, should there be a duplicate available in her absence?

It is now well known that computer experts, sometimes for fun and sometimes for malice, get access to other people's computer data or programs. One of the ways they can do this is by guessing passwords. Your name, the firm's name, the computer's name, your favourite cartoon character, are not secure passwords. The other well-known source of access to other people's computers is listening to conversations in the pub. So when you've thought up the best password in the world, don't brag about it.

It is also necessary to protect floppy disks from unauthorized access, and many storage boxes for disks have locks. Since physical damage to these records could also be disastrous, most people have instituted procedures to keep copies of their disks in a separate, secure place. Don't be casual about this – the one time you 'can't be bothered' is when something will happen.

Office gossip is a lot of fun in our daily lives, and the grapevine is a valuable source of information and communication. But, particularly when you are a new employee, do more listening than talking on it. Information you receive in the course of your work is confidential, and your employer should be able to rely on your discretion. If you should find out something that worries you because you think someone is behaving dishonestly or unethically, or that there is a question mark concerning the safety of yourself or other employees, speak about this honestly and frankly to your employer before you reveal it to outsiders.

34 *Outgoing Post*

In a large organization, all you may have to do to get a letter posted is to put it in the collection tray or take it to the post room. But even so, you may have to mark the envelope for first-class mail or airmail, and you should know something about the postage rates so that you are aware of the cost factor when you decide how to send something. Ask the people in the post room how they want you to mark letters (in many instances if a letter is not marked 'First Class' it will be sent second class, and if not marked 'Airmail' it will go by surface mail) and whether you should seal them; and find out the times of collection – particularly that of the last post for the day, so that you can be sure not to miss it.

The Post Office has leaflets telling you how to calculate the amount of postage needed for different weights and different classes of mail. There are also booklets which describe the other services offered by the Post Office, such as express delivery, special delivery, registered post, etc. You can always phone them and ask, too; or, if you think your firm might qualify for bulk rates because you send so much out, they can arrange to have one of their representatives call to discuss it with you.

Find out where your nearest post office is, and their hours of opening (sub-post offices often have an early closing day), in case you have to go to get stamps or post a parcel in a hurry. Also, the nearest posting box may not have a slot large enough for a big envelope, so you will have to take it to the post office counter. The last collection of the day from many post offices is around the close of the business day so, if you don't want today's letters to wait until tomorrow morning, you must know the time of this collection.

In a small firm you may have to take the responsibility for the post. You should always have enough stamps available, of the right denominations, and a procedure for getting money to buy stamps.

In many cases this will be done by taking money from the petty cash, making out a petty cash slip for the amount spent, and getting the post office clerk to stamp this as a receipt when you buy the stamps.

In a large office, where the post normally goes out through a central service, it may be a good idea to have a few stamps hidden away so that you can post a letter yourself if you miss the last collection of the day.

Many firms like to keep track of how much is spent each day on postage by listing in a postage book details of each outgoing letter or parcel and how much postage was put on it. You can then add up how much postage has been used in a particular period, or check to see that the stamps you bought were actually used on letters and did not disappear into thin air (which does sometimes seem to happen). Some businesses or professions also charge their clients for the cost of postage and, if this is the case with your firm, it is essential to keep track of each outgoing letter and its cost. A postage book also gives you a useful record as to which letters have gone out each day.

If you are in charge of sending out a small amount of post, you may find that the only aid you need is something to moisten the envelopes for sealing and the stamps for sticking. It is really a lot more comfortable than licking them, and some envelope glue has a taste that can last for hours. For this purpose, you can get a small plastic bottle with a sponge on top or a small sponge in a tray or a roller in a tray. In an emergency, you could use any moistened sponge or paper towel. If you have a large number of envelopes to seal at the same time, lay them out, open side up, with the flaps spread out so that each gummed strip is visible. Wipe the sponge over all the gummed flaps, and then start sealing down the envelopes, top one first.

If you send out anything larger than ordinary letters with one sheet of paper in them, you will also need a scale, unless you are prepared to take everything to the post office counter. Postage scales come in all sizes and capacities. The smallest will be suitable for checking letters only. Some postal scales indicate not only the weight, but do the work of calculating the amount of postage required for you. These either use a small internal calculator, or simply have a printed indication of the different postage rates at each weight. Obviously they need correction when the postage rates change; and if you are purchasing one, it is worth finding out how easy this correction will be, the next time it becomes necessary.

Before you seal the envelope or put it in the Out-tray: (i) make sure the letter is in the right envelope, and (ii) make sure the enclosures mentioned are enclosed. If you have a large enclosure, is the envelope big enough? When it is sealed, is it secure enough? It will have to take a certain amount of handling when going through the Post Office system and you don't want it to come undone. Add sticky tape or string if you feel it is at all necessary.

Postcodes help the Post Office to sort mail. Use them when you write to people, and take the trouble to add them to older entries in your address book or cards which might not have them already. The Post Office has a book of postcodes if you need to find them frequently.

Postage meters/franking machines

A franking machine prints the correct amount of postage on an envelope (or on a piece of tape to stick to a parcel). The meter part of the machine is taken to a post office, where a prearranged amount of postage is paid for in advance. And when this runs out, back the machine must go – so make sure that the procedures for checking on this are operating efficiently and that you aren't left with no credit in the meter at the last (or critical!) moment. There is normally a record book in which the amount of postage paid for each time is listed, so you can look back and see how often, on average, it has been necessary to buy more.

In the course of using the machine, it is necessary to set it for the amount of postage required, insert the envelope, and stamp it. In addition to stamping the amount of postage, there is usually a facility for printing a message or the name of the firm at the same time. Look at the different messages that you see on metered mail you receive.

In addition to the convenience of not having to lick stamps, there is the convenience of not having to store stamps securely, and of being able to put on the exact amount of postage needed, instead of finding that all the stamps you have left are six twenties and seven twelves when what you need is 28p. However, there is the initial expense of the necessary equipment, and the obligation to purchase rather large amounts of postage in advance.

For large quantities of post, there are machines that will:

collate sets of papers

fold up papers to fit into envelopes

stuff the envelopes

seal the envelopes

put on the postage

or any combination of these.

There are a number of systems for addressing large quantities of envelopes (or labels). Some store the addresses on computers or word processors, some have a metal plate (you have to send new addresses or corrections to a firm that makes these plates), some operate by a small card on to which you type the name and address. If you are in charge of such a system, you will first be shown how to use it, but thereafter you must make yourself responsible for keeping the information up to date by making changes or additions as necessary.

If you have a copier, one way is to type a list of names and addresses on to a form, usually two or three columns of addresses to an A4 page. You then put special pages of labels into your photocopier (instead of blank paper) and copy the names and addresses on to the labels. So for a single typing of such a list, you can get any number of labels done whenever you wish.

Don't forget that there are other ways of getting things to people. Parcels can be sent by rail, by courier service, and locally by taxi or motorcycle messenger.

The *Post Office Guide* describes the Post Office's services and should be part of your reference shelf. Of particular interest are:

Datapost – an overnight courier service

Expresspost – an express door-to-door delivery service

Swiftair – a worldwide express service.

Make sure you know about Post Office services such as recorded delivery (the recipient has to sign to acknowledge receiving the letter), registered post (the recipient signs, and the Post Office will insure the contents), express, etc. Read their brochures and remember to ring or ask at the counter for any information you may need.

. . . and incoming

It is worth checking on the dates of the letters you receive, and if they are not of yesterday's date or the day before, or some reasonable date in relation to the distance they have come, check the postmark on the envelope and keep the envelope with the letter. (Some firms like to keep all envelopes anyway, at least for a few days, in case of any query.) It may be misleading to see a letter dated 3 September without knowing, by reference to the postmark, that it was not in fact posted until 7 September (after the weekend, perhaps) and not received until a week later.

Which brings us to the question of noting the date of receipt. Many firms make a note on all letters of the date received. Some places use a date stamp. If you do, you must make sure that the date is changed each morning or this attempt at efficiency will be confusing rather than helpful. Some people stamp each letter with a form which allows you to write in the date received, the name of the person to whom the letter has been given for action, and perhaps an indication of the file in which it will eventually be put.

It used to be common practice to keep an incoming post book, in which all letters received each day were listed, and a note made of the person they were given to, or simply the date when they were answered. Some people keep a book in which are listed all cheques or payments received.

Some firms keep a book to list incoming registered post (or recorded deliveries), to make sure these get to the actual addressee. When the postman brings a recorded letter, he will accept your signature on the receipt even though the letter is addressed to someone else in your firm. So you may need a procedure that will describe such a letter, and let you get a signature from the person it is addressed to when you deliver it to him.

If you have a boss whose briefcase appears to be a wastepaper basket and who can lose papers within an hour of receipt, it may be worth taking a copy of everything important before you give it to him. Or institute the practice of filing the original and giving him a copy for action. If you do this, make sure the copy is clearly marked: (a) that it is a copy (photocopiers are almost too good these days!) and (b) where you have put the original.

It may also be necessary to make copies of any correspondence which should be seen by more than one person. Again, note on the original that you have circulated the letter to various people. In some instances a document should be seen by several people, but it is not important enough (or too big) to photocopy and anyway there is no hurry; so the document itself is circulated to a number of people. A slip of paper is attached listing the names of the people who should see it. It is sent to the first person on the list, who will look at it, put a tick or initials alongside his name on the list, and send it on to the next person on the list – and so forth. This slip is called a 'circulation' or 'routing' slip, and some firms have them printed or photocopied. Often the same people are required to look at a certain class of document, and their names may be in order of priority – who should see it first – or just in alphabetical order. Having a form for this purpose means you are less likely to forget someone.

It is traditional to put the boss's mail on his desk each morning with the most important letters on top, the least important circulars at the bottom – and you might like to exercise a bit of discretion about the order in which he sees the good news and the bad news. Some offices have an In-tray or various categories of In-trays, such as 'for immediate attention' or 'do today' or 'pending matters'. If so, it's important to check these periodically to see if various matters have been attended to and can be removed. Don't just pile more on top each day. There are other ways of sorting the mail – perhaps into folders or in stacks in a certain place. Your boss may find it helpful if you clip a letter to its previous correspondence or file so that he can refer to it.

Mail is often received more than once a day, whether from the postman or through the internal system. Make sure your system of dealing with it can cope with these additional deliveries; for instance, if your boss thinks he has seen all the incoming post for that day in the morning, will he look in his In-tray again? How can you bring the later correspondence to his attention?

35 *Your Reference Shelf*

Keep together and accessible all manuals and instruction books for all your equipment.

Have available near the telephone the telephone directories for your area, any business or commercial directories (Yellow Pages) that are issued for your area, and the booklet of dialling codes supplied by BT. The current dialling codes booklet also gives overseas codes and time differences. Be sure you also have BT's latest leaflet showing charges.

Have a copy of the Post Office Guide, or at least the leaflets showing domestic and overseas postage rates.

It is a good idea to assemble (perhaps in a looseleaf book) a reference guide for your own office. You can keep copies of all form letters, sample documents so that you know how to lay them out again (such as minutes, contracts, etc.), any procedures you will have discovered about how to do things. Don't you wish someone had left one of these for you when you took over?

You will want to have a dictionary, both to check spellings and to make sure a word is being used correctly. Be sure you have an up-to-date dictionary – it's a nuisance if it doesn't contain new words or usages. Your dictionary doesn't have to be very old, for instance, to lack a useful definition of 'computer'. Try it.

For quick checking of spellings and word separations (where to put the hyphen at the end of a line), there are small books, often called spelling dictionaries, which just list the words without a definition.

A thesaurus is a reference book that suggests to you words similar to the one you are looking up. If you have used the word 'company' several times and want an alternative, you will be referred to a section containing such words as organization, firm, corporation, etc. All the words in a section are not exact synonyms, so care must be taken in selecting one – you may have to look it up in the dictionary to make sure it is entirely appropriate. An alternative is a dictionary of synonyms.

You may want a shorthand dictionary showing the forms of whichever system you use. If your hand staggered when asked to produce an outline for an unfamiliar word, look it up and practise it.

It is useful to have a street guide to your town, and perhaps a map of your area available. If you often have to direct people to your office, you might keep a supply of photocopies of the appropriate map or plan, with a big X on your building; you could also locate on it the nearest bus, train or tube stop, and give directions for drivers.

A gazetteer or atlas will help you locate unfamiliar places and find out how to spell them, too. If your boss travels by car, perhaps you should keep handy essential guidebooks with road maps. If train travel is frequent, do you have the latest timetables?

If you have to make restaurant reservations for lunches or dinners, perhaps you should keep a *Good Food Guide* or something similar, both to find the addresses and phone numbers of restaurants and to be able to make suggestions if asked.

If you often need to check the names of people in public office, or in public life, you may need a reference book. Your librarian or bookseller can tell you which is the appropriate reference work for your purposes. Some examples are *Who's Who* (several editions for different occupations), *Who Was Who* (prominent people no longer alive), *Whitaker's Almanack*, *Pears Cyclopaedia*, *Debrett's Peerage and Titles of Courtesy* – go and look at some of these in your library or bookshop and see if they would be useful for your work.

You may need to find specialized dictionaries or reference books for the business or profession of your company (medicine, architecture, leather goods, etc.). There are also many books on the use of the English language, on forms of address, on how to run a meeting, on spelling and punctuation, on brushing up your shorthand, typing or other office skills.

Final Comments

So there you have it – a little more than the basic equipment you will need to make the transition from shorthand typist, through junior secretary to senior secretary, and beyond.

The purpose of this book has been to disabuse you of any illusory notions you may have had, or have received from others, about what a secretary actually *is*; to help you with advice gleaned from many years' experience in all sorts and sizes of jobs; and, we hope, to amuse you from time to time as well.

Most of all, we would like to think that this book will encourage you to become a senior secretary, to expand your skills and knowledge, and to find satisfaction in a profession that is all too often considered to be a menial, nine-to-five stop-gap between school and marriage, but which in fact you can tailor exactly to your own interests, ambitions, abilities, extra-mural commitments – and which you can pick up again, more or less where you left off, even after a gap of several years.

And there are not many professions as flexible as that!

Useful Addresses

Unique Freelance Secretaries
with Unique Conference Services
766 Finchley Road
London NW11 7TH
01-455 8187 or 455 1266 or 455 2120
(Secretaries, conference staff, tape transcription, word processing)

Pitman Publishing Limited
(Periodicals Division)
128 Long Acre
London WC2E 9AN
01-379 7383
(Publishers of 'Memo' and 'Pitman 2000' shorthand magazines)

London Tourist Board and Convention Bureau
26 Grosvenor Gardens
London SW1W ODU
01-730 3450
(for visitors to London, conference assistance and associated useful contacts)

London Transport
55 Broadway
London SW1H 0BD
01-222 0033

Good Food Guide
14 Buckingham Street
London WC2N 6DS
01-839 1222
(published by Consumers' Association – useful for restaurants)

Hammersmith and West London College
Faculty of Business Studies
Gliddon Road
London W14 9BL
01-741 1688

Association of Medical Secretaries, Practice Administrators and Receptionists
Tavistock House North
Tavistock Square
London WC1H 9LN
01-387 6005

Association of Legal Secretaries
The Mill
Clymping Street
Clymping
near Littlehampton
West Sussex BN17 5RN
0903 714276

Institute of Legal Secretaries
Portland House
4 Great Portland Street
London W1N 5AA
01-580 0342

Norma Skemp Personnel Services
3rd floor, 10 Storey's Gate
London SW1P 3AY
01-222 5091

Directors' Secretaries Ltd
27 Old Bond Street
London W1
01-629 9323
or
6 Martin Lane
London EC4
01-629 9323

Index